I0835833

OUTLINES OF AN INDUSTRIAL SCIENCE.

OUTLINES OF AN INDUSTRIAL SCIENCE.

By DAVID SYME.

PHILADELPHIA:
HENRY CAREY BAIRD & CO.,
INDUSTRIAL PUBLISHERS, BOOKSELLERS, AND IMPORTERS.
1876.

PREFACE.

The following pages were written in hours snatched from a laborious profession, often at wide intervals apart, and generally after a long and exhausting day's work. They were afterwards put together, and partly rewritten, on shipboard, on my way here from the Antipodes. These conditions are not very favourable to that concentration and continuity of thought which a subject of the kind here treated of requires, and this must be my excuse for any defects that may be found in them, which, I have no doubt, are numerous enough.

There is only one thing I take credit for, and that is, that I have endeavoured to put my ideas in as concise a form as possible. There is not a paragraph, sentence, or word, not absolutely necessary to explain my meaning that I have retained, so that, if I do not succeed in convincing my readers, I shall, at all events, have the satisfaction of knowing that I have not wearied their patience.

I have to thank my friend Prof. T. E. Cliffe Leslie for his kindness in reading over the proof sheets, and for some valuable suggestions which he has made to me, although this must not be understood as implying that our views are perfectly in accord on all points.

D. S.

London,

November 1st, 1876.

CONTENTS.

PART I.—MATTER AND METHOD.

CHAPTER I.

THE SUBJECT-MATTER.

CHAPTER II.

THE METHOD OF INVESTIGATION.

CHAPTER III.

ALLEGED SUFFICIENCY OF SELF-INTEREST.

CHAPTER IV.

ON DEMAND AND SUPPLY.

CHAPTER V.

ON COMPETITION.

PART II.—PRINCIPLES.

CHAPTER VI.

INDUSTRIAL FORCES.

CHAPTER VII.

ON VALUE.

CHAPTER VIII.

ON PRICE.

CHAPTER IX.

ON PRICE (CONTINUED).

PART III.—RELATIONS.

CHAPTER X.

RELATION TO SOCIOLOGY.

CHAPTER XI.

RELATION TO ETHICS.

CHAPTER XII.

RELATION TO ART.

PART I.

MATTER AND METHOD.

OUTLINES

OF AN

INDUSTRIAL SCIENCE.

CHAPTER I.

THE SUBJECT-MATTER.

ANY large or comprehensive subject usually requires, in order that it may be conveniently or exhaustively treated in all its details, to be broken up into separate parts or divisions, and these again into other parts or subdivisions. Accordingly, in dealing with the Science of Man, which is certainly one of the largest and most comprehensive of subjects, it has been the practice heretofore to consider it under two main divisions; under the one is included all that refers to the physical, and under the other, all that refers to the mental side of man's nature. And, carrying out the mode of treatment here indicated, we have, on the physical side, the organic sciences—Physiology, Anatomy, and Organic Chemistry; and, on

Classification of subject.

the mental side, we have Psychology, Ethics, Politics, and what is termed Political Economy.

Mode of procedure.

Another question of primary importance in dealing with such a subject as that before us, is the mode of procedure, or the process of investigation to be pursued. The first step is to arrange those facts or phenomena which are of a homogeneous character into distinct groups or classes. Our subject being Man, we have, on the physical side, for instance, the phenomena of human existence, the structure of the human body, and the various chemical processes affecting the living organism, which are treated under Physiology, Anatomy, and Organic Chemistry respectively. On the mental side, on the other hand, we have the phenomena of cogitation, of human judgments, or of what are included under the terms conscience and moral sense, of social organization, and of industrial activity, which are treated of under Psychology, Ethics, Politics, and Political Economy respectively. It is with the phenomena of the latter class alone that I propose to deal in the present instance.

The subject-matter.

When we look around us, we find mankind actively and incessantly engaged in operations of various kinds, and all of them entailing labour of a more or less painful character. They plough, they sow, they reap. They clear forests, reclaim swamps, and change the face of nature. They make roads, construct bridges and railways. They build houses, workshops, and palaces. They cover the land with cities, and the sea with ships. They work up the raw material of the field, the forest, and the mine into finished manufactures, and carry these to the most distant places of the earth. And along with all this, there is a continual process of exchange of products carried on between man and man, and between one country and another. Every one is producing something that some one requires, and everything produced is exchanged for something else; commodities for services, services for commodities, and commodities for commodities. The whole human race appears to be perpetually occupied in making and unmaking, in buying and selling, in producing and consuming. And this process is going on from day to day, from year to year, from one generation to another, without intermission. Why this restlessness, this incessant activity, this enormous expenditure of human energy? These are the phenomena which constitute the subject-matter of that branch of the science of man which I venture to call INDUSTRIAL SCIENCE. We have a Science of Mental Action, a Science of Moral Action, and a Science of Social Action; why should there not be also a Science of Industrial Action? On the other hand, it is difficult to see why there should be a science of Wealth. Why of Wealth any more than of any other object of human desire, as, for instance, of Health, of Power, of Honour, or of Fame?

Here it is necessary to say something about the title of this work. I have adopted the term *Industrial Science* instead of *Political Economy*, because the former properly indicates the subject under investigation, which the latter does not. Words are misleading when they do not convey the meaning intended. The word *Economy* means the regulation of the house, or the judicious management of a man's property, and is so used both by Aristotle and Xenophon. In its modern English acceptation, it means frugality or parsimony. Its technical or scientific use is, therefore, neither in accordance with the Greek nor English meaning of the word. Nor does the adjunct *Political* help us in the least out of the difficulty. In the first place, the qualifying word has already been appropriated by a cognate science (Politics) in strict accordance with its meaning. In the second place, when it is used as an adjunct to the word *Economy*, it conveys a false meaning, and one never intended by those who use it; for *Political Economy* would then mean the regulation of the house applied to the state. The term would express that management which the state exercises, or ought to exercise, for the benefit of all its citizens. I need hardly say that economists, and least of all those of the modern English school, do not inculcate the doctrine that the state should direct the industry of the country, which is the obvious meaning of the words. As, therefore, the term now used is misleading, even when applied to the subjects usually discussed under that head, and as it is even less appropriate to the scope of the following inquiry, I have preferred the term

The term *Political Economy.*

Industrial Science, as being more suitable every way considered.

Definitions of the Science.

Political Economy has been variously defined as "the science which states the laws regulating the production and distribution of wealth;"[1] "the science of the laws which regulate the production, accumulation, distribution, and consumption of those articles or products that are necessary, useful, or agreeable to man;"[2] the science which investigates "the nature of wealth, and the laws of its production and distribution."[3] The subject-matter of Political Economy, according to these authorities, is Wealth; and Political Economy may be said to be, and is, in fact, usually called, the Science of Wealth. Thus, Adam Smith discussed the principles of Economic Science under the title of *The Wealth of Nations*; and Prof. Hearn, more recently, treated the same subject under the title of *Plutology*.

The term *Wealth*.

It will be observed that in these definitions economic writers use the term Wealth in a purely technical sense. They understand by it all objects whatsoever which possess value.[4] With Malthus, Wealth includes "all material objects which are voluntarily appropriated by individuals."[5] McCulloch, as we have seen, does not employ the term Wealth, but uses the

[1] Senior, *Introductory Lectures on Political Economy*, p. 36.
[2] McCulloch, *Principles of Political Economy*, p. 1.
[3] Mill, *Principles of Political Economy*, p. 1.
[4] Senior, *Political Economy*, p. 6. Fourth edition.
[5] *Principles of Political Economy*, p. 33. Second edition.

periphrasis, "articles or products that are necessary, useful, or agreeable to man," to express the same idea; and Mill includes under it "all useful or agreeable things which possess exchangeable value; or, in other words, all useful or agreeable things, except those which can be obtained, in the quantity desired, without labour or sacrifice."[1]

Note here the difficulty which besets the student at the very outset of the inquiry, owing to the want of proper terms to express the subject-matter under investigation. First, we have the term *Political Economy*, which is either meaningless or misleading. Next we have to fall back on the term *Wealth* to indicate the subject-matter; but this, like the term *Political Economy*, is used in a purely technical sense, which is neither in accordance with its etymological nor its popular meaning. Surely no science was ever so unfortunately placed for want of a proper vocabulary. The terms *Political Economy* and *Wealth*, in the sense used by economic writers, violate nearly the whole of the seven fundamental aphorisms laid down by Whewell for the use of technical terms.[2]

---

[1] *Principles of Political Economy.* Preliminary Remarks, p. 11.

[2] Take for instance the last four:—

"4. When common words are appropriated as technical terms, their meaning and relations in common use should be retained as far as can conveniently be done.

"5. When common words are appropriated as technical terms, their meaning may be modified, and must be rigorously fixed.

"6. When common words are appropriated as technical terms, this must be done so that they are not ambiguous in their application.

In immediate connection with this difficulty there rises the question, Is Wealth, in the economic sense of the term, really the subject-matter of Political Economy? If so, and if Wealth consists, as we have seen it defined, of all objects necessary, useful, or agreeable to man, then Political Economy must be a very comprehensive science indeed, for there is scarcely an object that can be mentioned the possession of which is not more or less necessary, useful, or agreeable to some one, somewhere, at one time or other; and if, as J. S. Mill and his followers tell us, it is the object of Political Economy to investigate the nature of the laws which regulate the production and distribution (and, according to some, even the accumulation and consumption) of all things which constitute Wealth, there would absolutely be no limit to the inquiry, which would embrace an investigation into the nature of, and the laws which govern, everything under the sun. It is evident that economic writers have never sufficiently considered the import of this definition, or they could not have put it forth to the world in the manner they have done.

Is Wealth the subject-matter?

There is another consideration involved in this question. If Wealth consists of material objects (which no economic writer has yet called in question, although Mill would not limit his definition to these), then Political Economy

Is Political Economy a mental or a physical science?

"7. It is better to form new words as technical terms than to employ old ones in which the three last aphorisms cannot be complied with." *Dissert. on the Progress of Ethical Philosophy.* Works, vol. i. p. 5.

would be a physical and not a mental science. On the other hand, if Political Economy be a mental science, it has just as much concern with the objects which constitute wealth as Psychology, for instance, or Ethics has with the external world. It is a matter of the very greatest importance to have clear ideas on this point, as for want of them most writers on this subject have helplessly involved themselves in a maze of error.

The confusion of ideas we find existing, even amongst the most eminent authorities, as to the true character of Economic Science, is most remarkable. The only writers who have attempted to define the position of Political Economy are J. S. Mill and Prof. Cairnes, and neither of them has, it appears to me, succeeded in dealing with the subject in a satisfactory manner. "The laws of the production of the objects which constitute wealth," says Mill, "are the subject-matter both of Political Economy and of almost all the physical sciences. Such, however, of these laws as are purely laws of matter, belong to physical science, and to that exclusively. Such of these as are the laws of human mind, and no others, belong to Political Economy, which finally sums up the result of both combined."[1] It would be difficult to put together statements more irreconcilable with each other than those contained in the three sentences I have just quoted. "The laws of the objects

Mill's view.

[1] *Some Unsettled Questions of Political Economy*, p. 132.

which constitute wealth," we are told in the first sentence, "are the subject-matter of Political Economy" in common with all the physical sciences; in the second we are informed that only "such of these laws as are the laws of human mind" belong to this science; and in the third, notwithstanding we have just been informed that Political Economy has to deal with only a portion of these laws, it is stated, that it "finally sums up the result of both combined." One thing only is certain, that all three statements cannot be correct; for if Political Economy has to deal with the laws of matter, it cannot be a mental science; if, on the other hand, it has to deal with the laws of mind, it cannot be a physical science; and lastly, if it has to deal with both, it cannot be exclusively either the one or the other.

Cairnes's view.

Prof. Cairnes's explanation is, if possible, still more unintelligible. Political Economy is, according to this writer, "the science which, accepting as ultimate facts the principles of human nature and the physical laws of the external world, investigates the laws of the production and distribution of wealth, which results from their combined operation."[1] This definition is comprehensive enough if it has not the merit of clearness, and his remarks farther on do not help to simplify matters in the least. "The laws of the phenomena of wealth which belong to Political Economy to explain," he says, "depend equally

[1] *Character and Logical Method of Political Economy*, p. 10.

on physical and mental laws," and "the subject-matter of Political Economy, namely, wealth, is neither purely physical nor purely mental, but possesses a complex character equally derived from both departments of nature, and the laws of which are neither mental nor physical laws, though they are dependent, and, as I maintain, dependent equally, on the laws of matter and on those of mind." And again:—"Political Economy belongs neither to the department of physical nor that of mental inquiry, but occupies an intermediate position."[1] I confess I am unable to understand what these laws are which are neither physical nor mental; and I am equally at a loss to conceive the nature of the science which is here said to occupy an intermediate position between matter and mind.

Political Economy a mental science.

At this stage of the inquiry, I content myself with stating that I regard Political Economy as a purely mental science. When we consider that industrial phenomena are the product of human actions, and that human actions again are the product of mental impulses, no other conclusion appears to me to be possible. It is true that in treating of industrial phenomena we come into contact with material objects, but the fact does not necessarily make Political Economy a physical science. Even in the science of pure mind, we are constantly brought face to face with matter, as, for instance, when we trace ideas and sensations to certain external objects which produce them; but mental

[1] *Character and Logical Method of Political Economy*, p. 24.

science does not concern itself with the external objects, being occupied exclusively with the sensations and ideas of which they are merely the inciting cause. So it is with the material objects which constitute Wealth. It is not with these that Political Economy has to deal, but with the impressions which they produce, the mental associations connected with them, and the Desires which their presence or absence incite. Thus the presence of food produces a sensation of pleasure, and the absence of food a sensation of pain. The association connected in the mind with these sensations, and an object supposed to be capable of producing them, incite a desire to obtain possession of that object. These are all mental phenomena; and I maintain that it is with these, and with these exclusively, that Economic Science has to deal. Whether wheat, for instance, is a more nourishing article of human food than oats or barley, is no concern of the farmer who grows it, of the miller who grinds it, or of the baker who bakes it; the fact that wheat is an object of human desire is alone sufficient to ensure the expenditure of human labour in its production; and the various processes involved in its production, its conversion into flour and again into bread, form no part of the subject-matter of Economic Science, but belong properly to practical agriculture and domestic economy. The sole importance which this or any other object of Wealth has to the student of Economic Science, lies in the fact that it is, has been, or may become, an object of human desire.

Industrial Science defined.

The subject-matter of the science we have to investigate, therefore, is not Wealth, but Industrial Activity. Industrial Science may be defined as the science which investigates the laws which regulate human industry. Thus understood, Industrial Science is entitled to take its place among the mental sciences — a position to which Political Economy has hitherto been unable to lay any just claim.

CHAPTER II.

METHOD OF INVESTIGATION.

It is somewhat remarkable that so little attention has been given to the method of investigation in Economic Science. The modern English school, following Adam Smith and Mill, have, without exception, adopted the deductive method. Adam Smith, indeed, nowhere distinctly states what his method is, but from numerous remarks scattered throughout the *Wealth of Nations*, and from the whole tenor of that work, it seems tolerably certain that his treatment of the subject was mainly deductive. "The tendency of any man to follow his own interest," "the natural effort of every man to better his own condition," were fundamental propositions with him, and from these he deduced all the principles laid down in his work.[1]

Adam Smith's view.

Senior distinctly adopts the deductive method, and maintains that it is the only one applicable to the science.[2] "The general facts on which

Senior's view.

[1] See *Wealth of Nations*, book ii. ch. iii. See also book iv. ch. v.

[2] *Political Economy*, p. 1.

the science of Political Economy rests," he says, "are comprised in a few general propositions," of which the first and fundamental one is stated to be "that every man desires to obtain additional wealth with as little sacrifice as possible." By the desire for wealth, he explains, that he does not mean that everybody, or indeed anybody, wishes for an indefinite quantity of anything, or that wealth is, or ought to be, the principal object of human desire, but simply that no person ever feels his whole wants to be absolutely supplied, and that every one has some unsatisfied desires which he believes additional wealth would gratify. In his opinion, the proposition that "every man desires to obtain additional wealth," is self-evident; and he apologizes for explaining it at some length on the ground of its supreme importance, it being a proposition that is "assumed in every process of economic reasoning," is the "corner-stone of the doctrine of wages and profits, and, generally speaking, of exchange." In short, he maintains that the proposition is in Political Economy, "what gravitation is in physics, or the *dictum de omni et nullo* in logic: the ultimate fact beyond which reasoning cannot go, and of which almost every other proposition is merely an illustration."[1]

Cairnes's view.

I hardly know whether to include Prof. Cairnes among the deductionists or not, his views on the subject being so inconsistent. In his essay on *The Logical Method of Political Economy*, he evidently regards Political Economy as a purely deduc-

---

[1] *Political Economy*, p. 28.

tive science, although, strangely enough, he classifies it with Astronomy, Mechanics, Optics, Chemistry, and Electricity,[1] which are obviously inductive sciences; and in the same essay he describes it as "both a positive and a hypothetical science." In a more recent work,[2] however, he throughout discusses the subject from the standpoint of the deductionist.

Mill's view.

It is to J. S. Mill that we are indebted for the first clear and distinct exposition of the deductive method as applicable to Economic Science. "Political Economy," he tells us, "does not treat of the whole of man's nature as modified by the social state nor of the conduct of man in society. It is concerned with him solely as a being who desires to possess wealth, and who is capable of judging of the comparative efficacy of means of obtaining that end. It predicts only such of the phenomena of the social state as take place in consequence of the pursuit of wealth. It makes entire abstraction of every other human passion or motive, except those which may be regarded as perpetually antagonizing principles to the desire of wealth, namely, aversion to labour, and the desire of the present enjoyment of costly luxuries. . . . Political Economy considers mankind as occupied solely in acquiring and consuming wealth; and aims at showing what is the course of action into which mankind, living in a state of society, would be impelled, if that motive, except in the degree in which it is checked

[1] Page 40.

[2] *Essays on Political Economy*, Essay viii.

by the two perpetual counter motives above adverted to, were absolute ruler of all their actions."[1] The view here given, he goes on to explain, is not that mankind are in reality solely influenced by the motives referred to above, but that Political Economy is only concerned with these. It assumes that the desire to obtain wealth is "the main or acknowledged end" of industrial action, and it proceeds to treat of this as "the sole end." "There are," he says, "certain departments of human affairs, in which the acquisition of wealth is the main or acknowledged end. It is only of these that Political Economy takes notice. The manner in which it necessarily proceeds is that of treating the main and acknowledged end as if it were the sole end, which, of all hypotheses equally simple, is the nearest to the truth."[2] Mill here assumes, first, that "the main and acknowledged end" is the desire of wealth; secondly, that the main and acknowledged end is "the sole end." The process by which he converts a "main and acknowledged end," into "the sole end" is not discovered, so we cannot explain how the strange conversion has been brought about. It is not pretended that the second proposition is identical with the first, or that it is an axiomatic truth, or that it is based on what he calls "the real order of human affairs." He seems, in fact, to have assumed it on account of its simplicity, since the only reason assigned for its adoption is the statement that, "like all hypotheses

---

[1] *Some Unsettled Questions*, pp. 137, 138.

[2] Ibid. pp. 139, 140.

equally simple," it appeared to him to "be nearest the truth." In other words, the deductive method required an hypothesis, and this one appeared to him the most suitable for his purpose.

Mill's view examined.

This method has certainly the merit of great simplicity. Once admit the hypothesis, and the principles deducible from it become a mere matter of dialectics. An hypothesis to be of any value, however, must be capable of explaining all the phenomena for which it is used. Does the hypothesis in question serve such a purpose?

Strictly speaking, it cannot be said that the desire of wealth, in the sense of including purpose or end, is "the sole end" or motive of industrial action. A motive seldom or ever exists under conditions that admit of being regarded by itself. Generally speaking, every motive has more than one aspect or relation. There are intermediate, and there are ulterior ends. The acquisition of wealth cannot be regarded as an ulterior, but only as an intermediate end. Wealth is not pursued for its own sake, but on account of the pleasures it may bring, or the pains it may avert. The prospect of even an enormous amount of wealth will never impel to exertion if it is believed its possession would not conduce to happiness. Wealth is pursued as a means, not as an end; and the term "means" implies other modes of arriving at the same end, as the term "end" implies the subordination of means.

With regard to the hypothesis laid down by Mill, namely, that mankind invariably and exclusively act with a view to the possession of the maximum of wealth, with the minimum expenditure of labour or self-denial, I am surprised that it has been seriously entertained. Is it not within the experience of every one, that acts, of a strictly industrial character, are performed every hour of the day by persons into whose mind the idea of wealth has scarcely, if ever, entered? We do many things because other people do them; because we have become accustomed to do them; because by doing them we think we will gratify or benefit some one; and because we believe it right and proper they should be done. Even in cases where a decision has been arrived at after mature deliberation, the acquisition of wealth enters often as a merely subordinate consideration. A youth commences an industrial career by choosing a trade, business, or profession. Is his sole motive the acquisition of the maximum of wealth? If so, how is it that so many deliberately adopt a career that is comparatively non-lucrative? Or if it be said that it is his parents who choose for him, how is it that they do not invariably select the most lucrative?[1] When we see it stated,

[1] "What," asks Prof. Cliffe Leslie, "do we learn respecting the real division of employments in Auvergne—the motives which determine it, the distribution of landed property and other wealth, the scale of wages and prices—from the assumption that every individual pursues his pecuniary interest to the uttermost? Is it simply the desire of pecuniary gain which makes one Avergnat a porter at Lyons, another a priest at Clermont, and the sisters of both perhaps nuns, while an elder

with all the formality and scientific precision of an ascertained law, that the desire of wealth alone regulates profits, prices, and wages,[1] we naturally look for some evidence in support of the statement. But none is forthcoming. The statement is entirely unsupported by facts. It is a matter beyond dispute that profits, prices, and wages vary in different countries, and even in the same country and in localities immediately adjacent to each other, facts quite irreconcilable with the hypothesis that the sole motive of every man is to acquire the maximum of wealth. Take wages, for instance. The rate of wages in the same trade differs materially in England, France, Belgium, Germany, Switzerland, the United States of America, and in Australia. In no two of these

---

brother of each has the whole family property? In one only of the three regions described is pecuniary interest the dominant principle; and even in that region there are inequalities of wages and profits, with other economic phenomena, utterly with variance at doctrines which, by a curious combination of blunders, have been called by some writers, 'economic laws.' The faith of the school of English economists removes mountains. In France, where labour moves from place to place and from agriculture to other employments much more freely than in England, mountains certainly do not prevent the migration of labour. Yet even in France, the migration by no means takes place on such a scale, or with such facility, as nearly to equalize wages; and in places from which it is greatest, the department of the Creuse and the province of Auvergne, the main cause is not pecuniary interest. The younger brother in Auvergne goes from his home to a distant city in obedience to traditional family sentiments; and the peasant goes from Creuse to Paris as a mason, not because he has calculated the difference of earnings in the two places, and in different employments (for he could make more in many cases by remaining at home), but because his father went to Paris before him, and his comrades do around him." — *Fortnightly Review*, Dec. 1874.

[1] Senior, *Political Economy*, p. 28.

countries is the rate of wages the same. But the rate differs even in the same country. In some districts of France wages in the same trade are nearly double what they are in others. Every one knows that there are hardly two counties in England where the same rate of wages prevails. Agricultural labourers in the North get about 50 per cent. higher wages than the same class earn in the South and West.[1] There is a London rate, a Liverpool rate, a Manchester rate, and a Glasgow rate, in every trade. If the desire of wealth alone regulated wages, the workman would invariably migrate from those places where wages were low to those where they were high, and the rate would thus become uniform.

Perhaps the only place where an approach has been made to a realisation of this state of things is at England's antipodes. In the Australian colonies the labouring classes think nothing of undertaking a journey of hundreds, and even thousands, of miles in search of employment, for they pass freely from Victoria to Queensland, and even to New Zealand, and back, when wages are higher in the one place than the other; and when any new gold field is discovered in any part of Australia or New Zealand, they flock to it from all quarters by the thousand. But, then, all these colonies are under the same flag; the population are all of the same race; they all speak the same language; the

---

1 *Report of the Commission on the Employment of Children and Young Persons in Agriculture*, 1868. *Work and Wages*, by Thos. Brassey, p. 81. *Workmen and Wages*, by S. Ward, p. 156.

labouring classes have been inured to the nomadic life of the gold-digger, and few of them have any domestic ties of any kind; the people are so hospitable that a man can travel from colony to colony at very little expense, and, lastly, the climate is so genial that one may sleep in the open air for nine months in the year with perfect impunity. Elsewhere, however, the migration is of a very languid character, and a moment's consideration will show that it could not well be otherwise. A man has feelings, habits, and opinions which do not always harmonize with mere wealth-getting propensities. Early associations with his place of birth count for something with him; relatives, friends, and acquaintances bind him by strong ties to certain localities; and habits, which he cannot shake off at a moment's notice, make a frequent change of residence both unpleasant and inconvenient. He is, in fact, not the abstraction the deductionists represent him to be.[1]

---

[1] Curiously enough the elder Mill adopted a similar method in Politics to that which his son subsequently took in Political Economy. The former took as his postulate the proposition that all men desire Power, the latter that all men desire Wealth, and both worked out their conclusions in the same manner by deduction. (See *Essay on Government*, by James Mill, in collected *Essays*, p. 9.) No one knew better than the author of the *Analysis of the Human Mind*, that man has other desires than that of power, but he chose to ignore them on that occasion, and thereby exposed himself to Macaulay's merciless onslaught in the *Edinburgh Review*, which is now better known than *The Essay on Government* which called it forth. It is a remarkable instance of human inconsistency, that a process of reasoning which should at once be all but unanimously rejected, not only as unsuitable, but as absurd, when applied to one department of human nature, should, when applied to another, not only be looked upon as perfectly proper,

The maximum of wealth theory.

Let us see what would be the effect on industry if this hypothesis were correct. Suppose an employer and employé to be both influenced by the sole motive of obtaining the maximum of wealth with the minimum expenditure of labour or self-denial. The object of the employer is to get as much work done for as little money as possible; the object of the employé is to get the highest wages for the smallest possible amount of work. They agree, we shall suppose, as to terms; so much wages for so many hours' work. The workman knows nothing of what is implied by the word Duty any more than his employer; the social affections are not represented on the one side or the other; they have nothing in common between them but only this, that each is desirous of securing an advantage over the other. With the workman everything that he does is done grudgingly. His own and not his employer's interests are alone thought of. He takes no pride in his work; he never does anything but what he is compelled to do; and if he occasionally makes an extra effort he regards that only as so much loss. What would be the value of such services to an employer? The employer, of course, pursues a precisely similar course towards his workman. Each endeavours to cheat the other all he can, and sees no harm in it, for the only standard to guide them is their individual interests, and, according to this standard, what is good for the one is

---

but as the only possible method applicable, and should maintain its ground unchallenged for a quarter of a century.

bad for the other, and *vice versâ*. It is impossible to conceive of the existence of industrial activity under such conditions.

The single motive theory.

Equally impossible is it to conceive of the existence of society under such circumstances. A man of one idea is bad enough, but a man with one motive would become a pest to all around him, and a community of such individuals would become a pest to itself. There could be no responsibility in such a case, for the individual would be entirely uncontrollable in his actions. Even if the members of such a community were animated by the purest and most unselfish of motives, the desire to do good, the result would scarcely be an improvement on the present order of things. A society where every one was neglecting his own affairs and looking after the affairs of some one else, where no one had any personal wants or desires of his own to gratify, would be in a state of perpetual distraction. The members of such a society would be helpless as children in matters affecting themselves, and officiously intermeddling where they were not wanted. What, then, would be the case if all the members of a community were influenced by a single motive of an opposite kind? Suppose an individual actuated solely by the desire of wealth. That motive would take entire possession of him. He would be absolutely irresponsible for his actions. Every thought and act would be directed towards the acquisition of wealth, as the sole end and purpose of life. He would have no scruple as to the means of attaining this end. He would feel himself under no obligations to speak the truth, keep his promises, or carry out his engagements. If his end could be better or easier attained by cheating, robbery, and even murder, there is no reason why, according to this hypothesis, cheating, robbery, and murder should not be resorted to. The desire of wealth would become avarice in its most hideous form, and the individual under the control of this passion would become a danger to society. These are the phenomena that would manifest themselves if the hypothesis in question were the correct one; and the fact that such phenomena do not exist proves its worthlessness.

Even Mill admits his hypothesis to be inadequate.

While insisting that his hypothesis is the only correct one, Mill, nevertheless, shows his want of confidence in its truth by providing for the detection of errors, which he sees to be inseparable from its adoption. Political Economy, he tells us, inquires, "what are the actions which would be produced by this desire if, within the departments in question, it were unimpeded by any other. In this way, a nearer approach is obtained than would otherwise be practicable, to the real order of human affairs in these departments. This approximation is then to be corrected by making proper allowance for the effects of any impulses of a different description, which can be shown to interfere with the result in any particular case. . . . So far as it is known, or may be presumed, that the conduct of man in the pursuit of wealth is under the collateral influence of any other of the properties of our nature than the desire of obtaining the greatest quantity of wealth with the least labour and self-denial, the conclusions of Political Economy will so far fail of being applicable to the explanation or prediction of real events, until they are modified by a correct allowance for the degree of influence exercised by the other causes."[1] It must be admitted that the prospect of arriving at the truth by this process is not reassuring. For, in the first place, the fundamental hypothesis is admitted to be insufficient of itself, as only an "approximation" of the truth can be obtained by its application. In the second place, this approximation has to be corrected where other impulses "can be shown to interfere with the result in any particular case," while proof of such interference could only be shown by observation, or, in other words, by induction. Lastly, we presume, the "approximation" referred to has, when other motives intervene, to be corrected by adopting other kinds of hypotheses to suit particular cases, to be followed up independently in the same manner as the first. The result will only be an indefinite number of similar approximations. What is to be done with these when we get them? The conclusions arrived at by the first hypothesis, we are told, are to be modified by making a "correct allowance" for the degree of influence exercised by the other causes. But how, again, are we to ascertain "the degree of influence exercised" except by induction? and how are

[1] *Some Unsettled Questions*, p. 140.

we to arrive at the "antecedent causes" except by the same process?

He admits also the necessity of verification.

Not only does Mill admit that the results obtained by his peculiar process require to be corrected, he further admits the value of the inductive method in verifying the results arrived at by deduction. "We cannot," he says, "too carefully endeavour to verify our theory, by comparing, in the particular cases to which we have access, the results which it (the deductive method) would have led us to predict, with the most trustworthy accounts we can obtain from those which have been actually realized. The discrepancy between our anticipations and the actual fact is often the only circumstance which would have drawn our attention to some important disturbing cause which we had overlooked. Nay, it oftens discloses to us errors in thought still more serious than the omission of what can with any propriety be termed a disturbing cause. It often reveals to us that the basis of our whole argument is insufficient; that the data from which we had reasoned comprise only a part, and not always the most important part, of the circumstances by which the result is really determined."[1] What does this mean if not the abandonment of the deductive method? If, but for this verifying process, our deductions might be all wrong, what value can we possibly attach to the deductive method so far as its application to industrial phenomena is concerned?

[1] *Some Unsettled Questions*, p. 154.

But, in truth, the making-allowance theory is not applicable in all cases. Motives are of various kinds, and impel to various, and even opposite, courses of action, according to their character. One motive impels to one kind of action, another motive to action of an entirely different kind. I owe a man a sum of money, and if I am influenced solely by a desire to obtain the maximum of wealth by the minimum of expenditure, I will refuse to pay it; if, on the other hand, I am actuated mainly by a sense of duty, I will pay what I owe whatever may be the consequences to myself. There can be no compromise between motives such as these, any more than there can be between a negative and an affirmative proposition, and there can, therefore, be no "proper allowances" made in such cases. It is not a question as to the extent of the modifying influence of one motive upon another, but of two motives which neutralize each other.

The proper-allowance theory inapplicable.

If, then, the hypothesis in question fails to explain all the phenomena of industrial life; if the results obtained by this process are only approximately true, and can only be true by making allowances for disturbing causes; and if, at the same time, it is found to be impossible to make these allowances, or to adjust motives which neutralize each other; and if, after all, the verifying or inductive process is still necessary to correct important, and even fundamental errors, arrived at by the deductive process, surely enough has been said to show that this method is inapplicable to the subject before us.

Conclusion from the whole.

The true method is the Inductive.

In all investigations of which Man is the subject, the only proper method of treatment is by induction. Psychology, Ethics, Politics, and Industrial Science, are all Sciences of Observation. By the latter term we understand experience in its widest sense, including a recognition of the internal facts of consciousness as well as the external facts of human activity. Mill, indeed, contends that experience is altogether inefficacious in the moral sciences. "In chemistry and natural philosophy," he says, "we can not only observe what happens under all the combination of circumstances which nature brings together, but we can also try an indefinite number of combinations. This we can seldom do in ethical, and scarcely ever in political, science. We, therefore, study nature under great disadvantages in these sciences; being confined by the limited number of experiments which take place (if we may so speak) of their own accord, without any preparation or management of ours; in circumstances, moreover, of great perplexity, and never perfectly known to us, and with the far greater part of the processes concealed from observation."[1] It is no doubt true that the student of Industrial Science cannot treat human beings as the chemist can treat inert matter, nor is it necessary he should. Experiments enough are already made to his hand, and all that is requisite is that he should collect and apply them. Thus, the changes brought about in seasons of scarcity and plenty, in

[1] *Some Unsettled Questions*, pp. 146, 147.

periods of adversity and prosperity, of stagnation and activity in trade or commerce, affect production and consumption, prices, wages, and currency in a variety of ways, and are indirect experiments of the very greatest value. But we can also "try an indefinite number of combinations." All changes we make in customs and excise duties, and in the mode of taxation, for example, are, in their very nature, experiments; and the whole course of legislation in banking, currency, usury, forestalling, wages, and combinations; our factory acts, health acts, licensing acts, insolvent acts, insurance, landlord and tenant, and master and servants acts; our corn laws, game laws, poor laws, patent, navigation, and sumptuary laws, are nothing but a long series of experiments, and we can extend these in any direction we think proper.

Is more applicable to moral than to physical science.

Nor can we agree with Mill in the opinion that in the investigation of the moral sciences, as compared with the physical, the student stands at any disadvantage whatever. Indeed, we believe quite the contrary to be the case. In the physical sciences, as has been well said, we can only interrogate nature by a slow and tedious process, for nature is mute; but in the moral sciences the object, man, is also the subject, and he is a conscious articulate being. He can explain his own feelings and describe the motives of his own acts.[1] In the

[1] Lewis, *On the Methods of Observations and Reasoning in Politics*, vol. i. p. 165. See also Bain, *Mental and Moral Science*, p. 223.

moral sciences, therefore, we get directly at the cause; in the physical only indirectly. The individual knows what motives impel him to action; he can also ascertain the motives which influence other people around him, for he can interrogate them, and they can answer; and he has, in addition, the actions themselves, which he can interpret in the same way as he can the phenomena of nature. There is, therefore, no special reason why the inductive method should not be applicable to the moral sciences, at least in the first instance. Once the facts have been correctly ascertained, deductive reasoning may be founded on them, but not before. Deduction properly begins where induction ends.

CHAPTER III.

ALLEGED SUFFICIENCY OF SELF-INTEREST.

The dogma stated.

The principle that underlies the whole system of the English school of Political Economy is self-interest. This is regarded not only as an essential force, but as an all-sufficient one. It needs no supplementing, and it brooks no interference. So far from requiring to be adjusted or regulated by any other force, it is the grand regulator of all other forces. What wonder, then, that writers of this school never tire of expatiating on the great and manifold blessings which flow from this principle, that the very contemplation of these fill their minds with awe and admiration, till language almost fails to express the benign feelings with which it inspires them? Its existence, according to the writers referred to, betokens a wise and beneficent arrangement of Providence.[1] It is a sublime contrivance which indicates the benevolent purposes of the Deity.[2] Only let it have full scope, and wealth and

[1] Whateley, *Lectures on Political Economy*, p. 103.
[2] Bowen, *Principles of Political Economy*, p. 120.

prosperity, such as the world has never seen, will follow in its course. Like the rain from heaven, it sheds its blessing on the just and on the unjust. A man has only to pay exclusive regard to his own interests, and to be totally oblivious of the interests of every one around him, and he will infallibly ensure the good of all. The purely selfish man is a benefactor to his species in spite of himself. "A gain to each is a gain to all," as Bastiat tersely puts it. "The grand, the noble theorem, expounded by political economists, is this," says Mr. Newman, "that the laws of the market which individual interests generate, are precisely those which tend best to the universal benefit."[1] McCulloch even goes so far as to blame Adam Smith for not speaking in more glowing terms of his favourite principle; for not saying, in fact, that in promoting such branches of industry as are most advantageous to themselves, individuals "necessarily promote such as are, at the same time, most advantageous to the public."[2] But the blame was quite undeserved, for Adam Smith said very much in effect what McCulloch blamed him for not saying. "The effort of every man to better his condition" is, according to Adam Smith, "so powerful a principle that it alone, and without any assistance, is capable of carrying society to wealth and prosperity."[3] This is putting the matter quite strong enough, surely; but if self-interest be so

---

[1] *Lectures on Political Economy*, p. 63.

[2] *Principles of Political Economy*. Introduction.

[3] *Wealth of Nations*, book iv. ch. v.

omnipotent, and withal, so beneficent a principle, it must obviously have been a mistake to endow mankind with other dispositions that might interfere with it. The sentiments of justice, courage, fortitude, benevolence, and such like, which we affect to value so much, would, in such a case, not only be unnecessary, but, so far as they interfere with the beneficent operation of self-interest, positively pernicious.

Not in accordance with the laws of man's nature.

This dogma, on examination, scarcely accords with modern scientific ideas of man's nature. Those who adopt it have lost sight of the fact, that man is endowed with a constitution which subjects him to the operation of other laws besides those which, we are gravely told, are neither mental nor physical, but are for the occasion termed economic. The human organism being composed of certain physical elements, is subject to the operation of physical laws, as, for instance, the law of gravitation, and the law of chemical affinity; it is also subject to organic laws, as those of nutrition, of reproduction, of growth, and decay; it is also subject to mental laws, as those of cogitation and volition. Mental laws do not supersede organic laws, nor do organic supersede physical laws, but each class operates in its own sphere, simultaneously and independently. To say, therefore, that self-interest—the desire of wealth, or the desire of every man to better his condition, or by whatever name it is called—is alone sufficient to lead individuals and nations to wealth and prosperity, is equivalent to saying not only that a single motive is to supersede all other impulses, desires, or sentiments whatever, but all physical and organic forces as well, so far at least as the economic well-being of mankind is concerned.

But, further, those who contend for the sufficiency of self-interest in industrial action seem to forget that some people desire to prosper, and appear indeed for a while to prosper, at other people's expense; that, in fact, there are thieves and cheats in the world; that a large, and even respectable, so far as respectability now goes, section of the community make their living, and even fortunes and titles, by making and selling fabrics that are guaranteed not to wear, by making and selling goods that are short of their proper weight or measure, and by making and selling adulterated food, drink, and even drugs that kill when they ought to cure.

Nor with facts.

As the so-called laws of Political Economy, as expounded by this school, are simply an exposition of the mode in which self-interest operates, I propose, in the two following chapters, to discuss at some length the tendency of this force.

CHAPTER IV.

DEMAND AND SUPPLY.

Difference between this and competition.

Demand and Supply is different from Competition, though they are generally spoken of as one and the same thing. Strictly speaking, Demand and Supply indicates the relation between a buyer and a seller, or between a seller and a buyer, whereas Competition indicates the relation between two or more buyers and a seller, or two or more sellers and a buyer. Demand and Supply has reference to the exchange of two articles between two or more persons; Competition has also reference to exchange, but is complicated by demand on the part of two or more persons for the same article. Demand and Supply is a simple process of exchange; Competition is a double process, as there is first the struggle among competitors for the article and afterwards the exchange of it. Thus, when one person desires to buy an article and another desires to sell, exchange is said to be regulated by Demand and Supply; but when two or more persons desire to buy the same article, and only one person desires to sell, the two or more buyers have first to settle their differences amongst themselves, and subsequently with the seller, and thus exchange becomes complicated by the element of Competition.

Meaning of the term *Demand.*

Here it may be necessary to explain the meaning of the terms *Demand* and *Supply*. By *Demand* Mill understands the "desire combined with a power to purchase," or, as Adam Smith called it, "effectual demand," and by *Supply*, "the quantity of any commodity offered for sale."[1] But why should we speak of "effectual demand" any more than of "effectual supply"? In every case of sale and purchase there is an act of exchange, and in every act of exchange both parties to it stand in the same relation to each other, and both are supposed to be mutually benefited by the transaction. A beggar, says Adam Smith, may desire a diamond, but his desire would not be effectual if he had not the means of purchasing it; and this reasoning is endorsed by both Mill and Thornton. Practically, however, a desire must always be considered as combined with a power. The desire of the beggar for the diamond would be "effectual demand" if no one desired to possess it but himself. The desire, to be "effectual," must be capable of satisfying the desire of the holder, and nothing more, and a beggar may be as capable of doing this as any one else. "Effectual demand" is a demand on the one side that is related to a demand on the other;

[1] *Principles*, vol. i. book iii. ch. ii. 3.

that is to say, it is Correlative Demand. If another man offered more for the diamond than the beggar was able to give, the exchange, if effected, would then have been determined by Competition.

It is difficult to understand what is really meant by "effectual demand," or what purpose is served by the adoption of the term. Does it mean demand *effected*, that is, commodities actually purchased? Or does it only mean demand *capable* of being effected? If the latter, how can it be ascertained when a demand is capable of being effected except by the test of the market, in other words, by actual sale? Anything short of this would not be effectual, but only tentative. If the former, then "effectual demand" would cease to be demand at all as soon as a sale was effected. To add to the confusion, the correlative of "effectual demand" has been defined, as we have seen, "the quantity of a commodity offered for sale," which implies that the sale has not yet been effected. Clearly, the adjunct "effectual," if used at all, is as applicable to the seller as to the buyer; and if we are to suppose the desire to buy must be "combined with a power," so also must the desire to sell, that is to say, that the seller may have to come down to the price fixed by the buyer, as well as the buyer come up to the price fixed by the seller. If the seller demands too much he will have to lower his price to the demand of the buyer, precisely in the same way as the buyer, if he offers too little, will have to raise his price to the demand of the seller.

Corollaries from this law.

With regard to the mode in which Demand and Supply, or, as I prefer it, Correlative Demand operates, I have to observe, first, that the ability to purchase an article does not increase with the demand for it. On the contrary, the very strength or intensity of a desire may be a bar to its satisfaction by increasing the difficulty of purchasing. A starving man may have an overwhelming desire to purchase food, but he will not obtain it by desiring; he must have the means of satisfying the man who has it. Secondly, the ability to purchase is often in inverse ratio to the desire. The man who has a commodity he is not particularly desirous of selling, possesses a power over another man who has an intense desire to purchase it of him; intense desire is, indeed, often incompatible with the power to purchase, or otherwise, if the power existed, the desire would at once be gratified.

It ignores moral distinctions.

If these propositions be true, the real nature of Demand and Supply will be apparent enough. Demand and Supply is not essentially just, for it recognizes no moral distinctions. It is not universally and invariably beneficent, for it ignores the difference between wants and desires—a difference which is of the highest importance from an ethical point of view. A want differs from a desire inasmuch as the latter implies the alternative of abstinence, which the former does not. A want is a necessity; a desire is a superfluity, the gratification of which may be dispensed with. The demand for the conveniences and luxuries of life may, or may not, be complied with; the demand for subsistence is imperative, and permits of no alternative. Wants and desires, therefore, can never exchange on equal terms.

Contest between wants and desires.

Is the contest between wants and desires? Then the desires will be the gainer and the wants the loser. As a want is stronger than a desire, a man will sacrifice more for the satisfaction of the former than he will for the latter. The greater the want the greater the sacrifice; the less the desire the less the sacrifice. A starving man wants food, and another man has plenty of it, but no want, only a desire to make the best bargain he can. But the want must exchange with the desire, and the starving man may have to sacrifice all he has in order to satisfy the demand of the man who possesses what he requires. A famine occurred in Orissa in 1866, and the British authorities made the stupendous blunder of acting on the law of Demand and Supply in the case of the starving millions. They measured the wants of the famine-stricken inhabitants with the desires of the traders and merchants. It was contrary to the principles of Political Economy, forsooth, to interfere with the course of trade.[1]

[1] It is beyond dispute that the Board of Revenue in Calcutta had intimation of the approaching scarcity in Orissa. The famine occurred early in 1866, and in October, 1865, Mr. Barlow, at Pooree, ventured to suggest to the Board that the Government should import large quantities of rice to avert the horrors of famine, but the Board declined to interfere, distinctly alleging as their reason that such a course "would be contrary to the principles of political economy." Later on, when the inhabitants

This is not the only instance on record, but it is the most prominent in recent times, where a government has based its policy on the law of Demand and Supply; but I venture to hope that it will be the last time it will be attempted by a British government. In 1874, when a famine was threatened in Lower Bengal, the British authorities adopted a different policy from that carried out in Orissa in such a relentless manner a few years previously.

Contest between desires.

Is it a question of exchange? The holder of the commodity will endeavour to gauge the strength of the desire of the intending purchaser, and if he thinks the latter is very desirous of purchasing, he will demand a high price; if he believes the commodity is a prime necessity to him, that he must have it, and cannot purchase it elsewhere, he will extract the very highest price out of him that he can. The intending purchaser, on the other hand, is perfectly well aware of the mental process going on in the mind of the holder, and acts accordingly. He tries to make it appear that he is not particularly anxious to purchase; that, in fact, it is quite a matter of indifference to him whether he does so or not, knowing well that if he allowed the other to

---

were dying at the rate of 4000 a week, and the Board had again been urged to do something, they made the following *memorandum*:—"On general grounds they (the Board) had a very strong objection to interfere with the course of trade." Again, in May following, when the famine was at its height, in answer to another remonstrance from the local authorities, the Board replied that "it (the famine) may be safely left to produce its own effect;" and produce its own effect it did, for a million and a quarter of human beings died of starvation.

understand that he had no alternative but to purchase, he would have to pay an exorbitantly high price.

Is it a question of wages? The weaker side suffers again. An employer wishes to increase his profits, and he looks around him to see where he can effect a reduction in his expenditure. He decides on reducing the wages of his men, because he believes he can take them at a disadvantage. Accordingly he waits his opportunity. This arrives when there are indications of a dullness of trade, and at once he discharges a number of men as a preliminary, giving the rest notice that their wages will be reduced. The men submit because they think they cannot help themselves, the action taken by their employer having impressed them with the belief that they are not indispensable to him. The workmen, on the other hand, adopt the same kind of tactics when they demand an increase. They do not make this demand when business is dull, as it might be a convenience rather than otherwise to their employer if they left his establishment at such a time. Their opportunity for striking with effect arrives when business is brisk and profits high, for at such a time their employer will rather concede their demand than run the risk of losing his profits. And the workmen, when their trades union have determined on an increase, are also very circumspect in their selection of a first victim. They do not attempt to try conclusions, at all events in the first instance, with an employer who has ample means of resisting them, or if they do, it is at a

Illustrated by the case of a wages dispute.

time when he has time contracts on hand; but they carefully select a man of straw, and with whom the stoppage of business, even for a day, would be ruin. An employer under such circumstances cannot help himself, and succumbs at once.

All attempts to settle the wages difficulty by Supply and Demand have hitherto ignominiously failed. If capital take advantage of labour at one time, labour takes advantage of capital at another. To-day it is labour that is down, to-morrow it is capital; and so the conflict is perpetually renewed. The difficulty will never be got rid of till we come back to first principles. In all disputes of this nature the claims of capital and of labour should both be taken into consideration and equitably adjusted. The question with the employer should not be how little can he compel his workmen to take, or with the workman how much can he get out of his employer; but the question with each should be what would be fair and equitable to both the one and the other. The true solution of the wages difficulty is to be found in the Courts of Arbitration, where the principles I contend for are fully acted upon.

Effect of on the rate of wages.

It is a well-established fact that when the demand for employment is in excess of the demand for labour, wages fall. The excess may be due to various causes, which we need not here enumerate. But let us suppose it is due to an increase in the number of labourers from reproduction. The increase in this case, then, would be due to an organic law. But why should this affect the rate of wages? What necessary connection is there between the number of labourers and the rate at which their services are remunerated? The means of payments, the so-called wages-fund, is, in the case supposed, not encroached upon in any way. The employers of labour are not in the least affected; their profits are not reduced, and they bear no share of the expense of maintaining the additional number of labourers. It is the contest again between wants and desires. The labourers demand employment, the employers demand labour; but as the labourers' wants must be satisfied, they are compelled to sacrifice more than their employers, who have the alternative of abstinence which the labourers have not. The labourers feel the pinch of hunger and they give more work than before for the same remuneration, or take less remuneration for the same work. The justice or beneficence of this arrangement is not very apparent, for the employers, on the one hand, secure a gain which they did not earn, and the labourers, on the other, suffer a loss which they do not deserve, and at a time when they can least afford it. Nor is the expenditure in wages increased in consequence of the increase in the number of labourers. The amount expended will certainly be smaller instead of greater, unless employers extend their operations and so give employment to more hands, which they may, or may not, be able to do. Economic writers, however, assume that a greater amount would invariably be expended under such circumstances; and as they say this would necessarily be distributed among a larger number of persons, it is taken as another exemplification of the wise and beneficent purposes that are served by Demand and Supply.

Let us now suppose that the number of labourers still continues to increase. The supposition is not an improbable one, for apart altogether from the operation of organic law, an increase would take place from economic causes alone. In the first place, it is a well-ascertained fact that in periods of great industrial depression, the labouring classes suffer more severely than the classes who are removed above want, and that the class immediately above the very poorest, who obtain their living by ordinary manual labour, are almost invariably dragged down to the lowest level, and thereby help to swell the ranks of competitors for the ordinary kinds of employment. In the second place, the very fact that a man is unable, by his own individual exertions, to comfortably provide subsistence for himself and family, compels him to have recourse to the members of his own household in order to eke out a living, who thus become competitors with him for employment. It may be observed that in almost all the accounts of the earnings of the agricultural labourers in the South and West of England that have been published in the press from time to time, the wages of the wife and children are always included in those of the husband and father. If, then, the number of labourers continued in this way to increase, and the

Injurious effects of low wages.

demand for employment increased in proportion, as economists insist would be the case, employers would, as before, take advantages of the necessities of the labourers and reduce their wages till they might be insufficient for bare subsistence. In such a case the labourers would be less able to perform the duties required of them, and numbers of them would starve or become a charge on the community. Thus the effect would be in the highest degree injurious, whether regarded from a moral, social, or economical point of view. It would be injurious morally, because labour would be deprived of its just reward; it would be injurious socially, because the labourers would become a burden on society; and it would be injurious economically, because labour would become less efficient.

Argument from enlightened self-interest.

I may be told that enlightened self-interest would always prevent the occurrence of such a disastrous result as I have here indicated. But I am not so sure of this. Enlightened self-interest is still self-interest, qualify it as you will. "A human being, by cherishing interested associations, does not," says Mr. Bain, "as a matter of course attain to either justice or beneficence. Even the most far-sighted prudence, as regards self, would not develope the whole virtue of beneficence."[1] Enlightened self-

[1] Note to Mill's *Analysis*, vol. ii. p. 304. See also *Mental and Moral Science*, p. 240; Mill, *Fragments on Mackintosh*, pp. 51, 52, and Hume's *Essays*, vol. ii. p. 223, where the reality of moral distinctions is insisted on.

interest did not prevent the physical deterioration of the Spitalfields weavers, who are said to be rapidly dying out, and their children, or such of them as have survived the struggles of poverty in early life, are, according to the testimony of medical men in the eastern districts of London, exhibiting the usual signs of impaired constitutions, such as narrow chests, imperfect muscular development, and very faulty teeth. Enlightened self-interest did not prevent the over-working of women and children in factories, to the injury of their health, and the physical and moral well-being of the rising generation, for the early factory acts were passed in the face of the strongest opposition from the employers. Enlightened self-interest did not prevent the wages of agricultural labour in the south of England being reduced to such an extent as actually to deprive the labourers and their families of a sufficiency of nourishment to maintain them in health and vigour, as was proved in an inquiry instituted by the Government in 1863, and conducted by Mr. Simon, one of its own officers; and it did not save the poor needlewomen of London from pauperism, or worse, for the price paid for needle-work in the metropolis is, and has for years been so small, that competent authorities have declared that, work as hard as they may, the needlewomen are unable to earn what will obtain them the bare necessaries of life at their occupation, and they are thus forced to supplement their earnings by outdoor relief from the poor rates, or to adopt other and even less creditable means of obtaining a livelihood.[1] As long as the present supply of labour is kept up, employers, who regulate their conduct by the dictates of self-interest, will not sacrifice present gains for future prospects, and will seldom trouble themselves about the welfare of others.

The rate of wages in relation to the price of provisions.

Let us now see how Demand and Supply operates in seasons of scarcity. If self-interest were as beneficent in its operation as alleged, this is the very period when employment would be plentiful and wages high. But the very reverse is almost invariably the case; for when

[1] The subject of giving outdoor relief to this class of work-people was formally brought before the President of the Poor Law Board (Mr. Goschen) in December, 1869, who made a minute to this effect:—"It is illegal to administer relief so long as a person is in employment and wages are earned, though such wages may be insufficient. The Poor Law authorities ought to hold aloof and refuse to supplement the receipts of the family, actually offering in preference to take upon themselves the entire cost of their maintenance." To this minute the Holborn guardians replied as follows:—"The guardians do not wish to disguise the truth. They are convinced that it is by means of the relief afforded to the outdoor infirm and more or less disabled poor that the competition in the lower forms of labour is increased to such an extent as to reduce the wages paid for it. The price of various forms of needlework could not be maintained at the present starvation standard, but that so much is done by persons in the receipt of parochial relief. A pauper of middle age, unfit perhaps for any very active occupation, requires to sit at work for a remuneration which rarely exceeds one halfpenny per hour. A botching shoemaker ekes out his parish relief by wages which, with hard work, range from 4*d.* to 8*d.* per day; a needle-hand the same; a slop tailoress and renovator only a little more; and even the widow who goes out charing, though forced to take a lower and lower rate of wage according to the numbers in the district, is only enabled to do so under parish help."

provisions are scarce the price is high, and labour is ill rewarded. The cause of this is obvious enough. The high price of provisions increases the cost of living to all classes, employers as well as workmen. The employers, therefore, when they find their expenses increased, naturally enough endeavour to curtail them, and first the services of one man and then of another are seen to be unnecessary, and are accordingly dispensed with. The same thing occurs in domestic service. In households where three servants were formerly kept two only are now retained, and where there were two, an attempt is now made to do with only one. The result is that large numbers of work-people of both sexes are thrown out of employment. But this is not all. The fact that numbers are thrown out of employment affects also the rate of wages of those who are employed, for rather than go idle some will consent to take less wages, and what some will take others cannot refuse, and so the rate is reduced to those whose services are retained. The fact is indeed beyond dispute, that wages never rise in seasons of scarcity, but almost invariably fall.[1] The inevitable result is a wide-spread destitution among the mass of the community.

---

[1] See Tooke's *History of Prices*, vol. i. pp. 14, 226, 227, and note at p. 329; also vol. iii. pp. 51—53. On the other hand, a rise of wages almost always accompanies, or immediately follows, a fall in prices. In 1833-34-35, for example, the price of wheat was lower than it had been for 70 years previously, while employment was abundant and wages high.

Distinction between necessaries and luxuries.

This law of Demand and Supply operates to the disadvantage of the weaker side in a still more extraordinary way. The scarcity of food is due to the operation of physical laws; the sufferings of the poor are due to the operation of organic laws; but another law, a purely mental or economic one, now comes into operation and positively augments these sufferings. Economists point to the fact, as further illustrative of beneficent design, that when any commodity becomes scarce, the effect of the scarcity is mitigated by the high price now charged for it causing reduced consumption. This is no doubt correct in the case of ordinary commodities, but when the commodity is a necessary of life, as bread, for instance, the law is the reverse of beneficent, for, in this case, the increase in price in usually out of all proportion to the deficiency in the supply. The disproportion is explained on the principle that, this commodity being a necessary of life, the desire to purchase it becomes the more intense as the scarcity is felt; or, in other words, that the price is in proportion to the desire to purchase, and not in proportion to the deficiency of the supply. Dr. Chalmers has pointed out that when articles of luxury are scarce, the increase in price is never so high as in the case of the necessaries of life.[1] Wheat, for example, has been known to quadruple in price when the deficiency was only one half.[2] Now the

[1] *Christian and Economic Polity*, vol. ii. p. 252.

[2] See Tooke's *History of Prices*, vol. i. p. 12.

poorer classes are necessarily the greatest sufferers when the price of bread is high, as its purchase forms the chief part of their expenditure, and they actually increase the price upon themselves by the very intensity of their desires. Here, then, we have an economic law, which, so far from ameliorating the severity of natural laws, positively aggravates their severity.

Case of Mr. Milne.

Fortunately, we are not left to conjecture on this matter, for we are furnished with a well-authenticated case which illustrates the principle I am endeavouring to establish. In 1814 a Mr. Milne, a landowner, gave the following evidence before a Select Committee of the House of Lords, on the Corn Laws:— "I wished," he said, "to enclose a farm at the end of the year 1812, or in the beginning of 1813. I sent for my bailiff and told him that I had enclosed, about twenty-five years ago, a good deal of land; that the inclosure at that time cost 3*s.* 5*d.* per ell of 37 inches; that a neighbour of mine, two or three years ago, had made similar enclosures which cost him 5*s.* 5*d.* per ell; that I thought he had paid too much, and that I ought to do it cheaper. The answer I got from my bailiff was, that provisions were very high, that labourers were doing double work, and that of course there was less demand for labour, and that he could do these inclosures last year at a cheaper rate than I had ever done them, and he actually executed these inclosures at 2*s.* 6*d.* per ell. He again came to me and told me that I had proposed to him to do some ditching upon another farm, which I did not intend to do till about a twelvemonth, from the circumstance of not being fully in possession of the whole farm. He requested that I would allow him to do it that season, as he could do it so much cheaper, and that a great many labourers were idle from having little work, in consequence of those employed doing double work. I desired him to go on with that labour likewise, and he actually contracted for my large ditches at 6*d*. an ell, which I do not think I could now do under from 1*s*. to 1*s*. 6*d*., in consequence of the fall in provisions." Here we have, as in the case supposed, the joint operation of physical, organic, and economic laws. Now note the operation of the latter on the two former. Food is scarce and dear, but employment instead of being more plentiful is less so. Owing to the high price of food, employers curtail their expenses, and labour being less in demand and the demand for employment increased, wages fall. But, unlike the employers, the labourers cannot adopt the alternative of abstinence; they cannot do without food, and to obtain this they must find employment. Food being dear, and employment scarce and more in demand than formerly, the condition of the labourers is aggravated by their very necessities. They not only compete among themselves for what little employment is offered, and consequently help by their own act to reduce wages still lower, but they now do double the amount of work for less remuneration than they obtained when provisions were cheap, and thereby actually deprive other labourers of a share of what remains.

Different effects of on capital and labour.

One more illustration of economic beneficence, and I have done. It is a well-ascertained fact that when any commodity in general demand rises in price (money alone excepted, in regard to which the opposite effect takes place), the price of other commodities falls in proportion, owing to the fact that the income of consumers does not increase with the increase in prices. The consequence is, that when the price of a commodity of this description, say bread, is high, consumers economize in other directions, in order to make good the deficiency in their income caused by the additional expenditure on this particular article. There is, therefore, less demand for those other commodities, as well as for labour, which is a commodity in general demand, and the price of them consequently falls. The wealthy man, however, is scarcely affected by the high price of bread, as this forms only a small proportion of his expenditure, and the increase in price is, to a great extent, compensated by the fall in the price of the other commodities, labour included, which he purchases. But with the poor man the case is different. Bread being with him the chief article of expenditure, when the price is high it bears heavily on his income, while his labour, at the same time, shares in the general depreciation. Thus the poor suffer in two ways; first, in the increased price of the necessaries of life, and, secondly, in the decrease in the value of their labour.

These anomalies are all the more striking when we consider the relation of capital to labour. Capital is an instrument that costs nothing to keep; it is not subject to tear and wear; it never loses bulk, and if lent out at interest it doubles itself in the course of so many years. It is far otherwise with the instrument of labour. The labourer has to be maintained at considerable cost, whether earning wages or not; he has to make provision for sickness and old age, and the worn-out instrument has to be replaced. Whichever way we look at it, indeed, we shall find that capital has the advantage. The man whose necessities are great will have to pay more for what he requires than the man whose wants are less urgent. The trader of limited means, if he buys on credit, will be charged more for his goods than the man who has a good balance at his bankers. The poor man, who buys his necessaries in small quantities, will have to pay a higher price for them than the rich man who purchases on a larger scale. The less consideration a man requires the more he gets, and the more he needs the less is shown to him. In the economic world honesty counts as nothing, and help comes in the inverse order of a man's needs.

With such glaring inequalities staring them in the face, it is not to be wondered at that economic writers repudiate the idea that the principles of their science are in accordance with our notions of a just administration of the scheme of things. Prof. Cairnes, in his latest and most ambitious work, frankly confesses that he is unable to see, in the results flowing from the action of economic laws, any realization of the principles of abstract justice.[1]

[1] "I am unable to find in the maxims of abstract justice any key to the practical problems of the distribution of wealth; and I am bound to add that just as little can I discover in the actual results flowing from the action of economical laws a realization of the principles of abstract justice."—*Some Leading Questions of Political Economy*, p. 320.

Prof. Walker makes a similar admission:—"It cannot be controverted," he says, "that the tendency of purely economic forces is to widen the differences existing in the constitution of industrial society, and to subject any and every person and class of persons who may, from any cause, be at disadvantage in respect to selling his or their service or product, to constantly increasing burdens." — *The Wages Question*, p. 166.

CHAPTER V.

ON COMPETITION.

THE sufficiency of self-interest once granted, freedom of contract, or unrestricted Competition, follows as a matter of course, as it would be absurd to assert that this principle was all-sufficient, and at the same time set limits to its operation. Unrestricted competition is therefore regarded by the English school of economists as the foundation-stone of their whole system. Indeed, Mill goes so far as to say that it is only on this basis that Political Economy is entitled to be called a science.[1] This is a principle, therefore, that admits of no compromise with the disciples of this school; and it is but fair to say that, in theory at least, they have accepted it without the slightest reservation. With them Competition is the grand regulator of industrial action. It is "beneficent, just, and equalizing."[2] It is in the market of the world "what gravitation is in the

Sufficiency of self-interest implies unrestricted competition.

---

[1] *Principles*, vol. ii. book iv. ch. iv. 2.
[2] *Plutology*, p. 339.

mechanism of the heavens, an all-combining, all-balancing, and beneficent law."[1] It is "the most progressive, the most equalizing, and the most communistic of all the provisions to which Providence has confided the direction of human progress."[2] This language, however, is scarcely justified by facts, for there are many circumstances in which competition is the reverse of beneficent, just, or equalizing; and so far from its being the all-balancing, all-combining law they represent it to be, the principle itself is a provision which requires adjustment. Every one knows that excessive competition produces enormous waste, and that it leads to the perpetration of fraud, the extent of which is generally in proportion to the intensity or keenness of the competition.

The object of competition.

We shall get rid of the high-flowing sentiment that surrounds this subject as soon as we have ascertained what the object of competition really is. The vulgar idea is that the object of competition, or, at all events, one of its results, is to reduce prices. But this is neither its object nor a necessary effect of its operation, as a moment's consideration will show. Competitors do not desire to lower or to raise prices, but to obtain possession of something some one else has, and which some one else desires. Sellers compete in order to secure a market; buyers compete in order to secure possession of some commodity. There is nothing just

[1] Newman's *Lectures on Political Economy*, p. 119.

[2] Bastiat's *Harmonie Economique*, p. 407.

or beneficent in one man outbidding another for the possession of an article, or in underselling another in order to secure a purchaser or a market. In either case the successful competitor attains his end at the expense of his rival; and in neither case is it intended that others than himself should derive any benefit whatever from the transaction.

Custom, compe-tition, and co-oper-ation.

Competition may be better than custom (which, according to Mill, takes precedence of competition in the order of development), when the circumstances are changed under which the latter grew up. Co-operation, again, may be better than competition when the latter is carried to excess. But even co-operation, could we conceive it capable of universal application, can never be relied upon, for it rests mainly on self-interest, and a man can never be made to act more disinterestedly by being made more selfish. Custom, local or vested interest, or by whatever name it may be called, may be good in the earlier stage of industrial development, as, for instance, in the case of patents and rights which are always granted for a limited time; competition may be good in a more advanced stage; and co-operation may, in a still higher stage, be better than either; but they are all mere expedients, provisions, or methods of carrying out the principles of fair dealing, and which, like the ceremonial law when it has lost its symbolic meaning, or positive law when interpreted according to the letter and not according to the spirit, are liable to abuse, and only act beneficially when they express the true ethical sentiment. If sellers never demanded more than a fair profit on their goods, they would have fewer competitors to contend with, there would be less dishonest rivalry, and the public would be better served.[1] There can be little doubt that the enormous profits often demanded provokes excessive competition, and excessive competition leads to the dishonest practices which disgrace modern commerce. The fact that sellers are ready to take less for their goods than they demand proves that they asked too much in the first instance, and the existence of excessive competition in any branch of trade is presumptive evidence that the profits in that trade have at one time been exorbitant. When the moral tone of the community is raised, when it is considered dishonourable to have two prices for the same article, and when a seller takes it as a personal insult to be asked to take less for a commodity than he demands, competition will wear a very different aspect from what it does at present.

Tendency of competition.

It is quite a mistake to suppose that competition invariably tends to reduce prices. It is only when sellers compete that prices are lowered, for when buyers compete they are invariably raised. The object of the producer in engaging in any

[1] Prof. Cairnes asserts that there is a far greater amount of competition in the wholesale than in the retail trade, owing to the fact that retail dealers have fixed prices while the wholesale dealers have not, the former resting, as he says, "upon a moral rather than an economical basis," and he adds that the result is to "the advantage of all concerned."—*Some Leading Questions*, p. 128-130.

branch of industry being profit, he will naturally take all the means at his command to increase that profit to the utmost. But a man will be able to make a larger profit if he has the whole market to himself than if he shared it with another, and, as a rule, the greater the amount of competition in a given market, the smaller will be the amount of profit to be divided among the competitors. It will thus become the object of every competitor to reduce the number of his rivals. The tendency of competition will therefore be in the direction of monopoly. A monopoly is said to exist when one man, or several acting together, hold entire possession of any commodity, or control any market. Competition exists when possession is disputed. If competitors, however, act exclusively with a view to their own interests, as we are told they must, it will be their main object to reduce competition to a minimum, or, in other words, to create a monopoly. Thus the principle from which the deductionist started, namely, the sufficiency of self-interest, instead of tending to competition, leads back ultimately to restriction in its worst possible form.

Conditions necessary to annihilate competition.

The profits of producers are largest when consumption is in excess of production, and the prospect of sharing in these induces competition. When production overtakes consumption, profits are reduced, and no more competitors enter the field. When production is in excess of consumption, and competition goes on as before, profits may cease altogether, and then begins the struggle for existence among competitors. Each competitor will now endeavour to obtain the customers of the others, by fair means or foul, and the inevitable result will be that strength and cunning, as in the animal world, will prevail, while the weak and honest trader will go to the wall. In order to render competition successful, in other words, to establish a monopoly, one of two things, or both, are requisite on the part of a competitor. The first is the command of a large capital; the second is the absence of all moral principle.

The first condition, capital.

As in a physical contest a strong man will, other things being equal, overcome a weak one, so in any industrial contest the man of large capital will inevitably overcome the man of small means. The large capitalist has the game in his own hands. He can arrange his mode of attack, and fix the day of victory. All he has to do, if a seller, is to undersell his rival, and the lower he fixes his prices the sooner he accomplishes his purpose. If he sells at a loss, so much the better, for then the resources of his rival will be all the sooner exhausted. It is a simple question of figures. If A has a capital of £10,000, and B who enters the field against him has a capital of £50,000, B's capital will outlast A's in the proportion of five to one; that is to say, B's chances of success will be five times better than A's. In such contests there are, of course, other conditions which go far to counterbalance the advantages of large capital, but in the present instance we are supposing these to be absent, and that both start on equal terms in every respect except as regards capital.

The case where capitals are unequal.

We are all familiar with the process which takes place when rival lines of coaches run on the same road. The first result is a reduction of the fares, commenced by one of the competitors, and followed sooner or later by the other; then other reductions follow till the traffic is carried on at a loss. When this point is reached, the matter becomes simply a contest between two capitals, in which the largest is sure to win. In carrying on the traffic at a loss, neither of the rival capitalists, however, has the slightest idea of benefiting the public, and, in the long run, the public will certainly not derive the slightest benefit from the contest, but rather the reverse, for the successful competitor, that is, the one who has established a monopoly, will take good care to recoup himself when the contest is over for all the losses he may have sustained while carrying it on. Thus the public, while they imagined they were getting an advantage from the low fares, were only assisting in creating a monopoly against themselves, all the cost of establishing which will ultimately come out of their own pockets.

The case where capitals are equal.

This is the ordinary result of competition when one of the competitors has the command of a larger capital than is possessed by the others. When, however, the capitals of competitors are more equal, and especially when they have each sunk a large portion of it in starting the business, competitors do not usually resort to the exhaustive process of crushing out one another, since they may attain their end by more direct means. Knowing that, in order to compete successfully, one or other of them must lose all his capital, they soon discover another method of achieving their object. The question being simply one of profit, the only matter for consideration with them is, Which is the most profitable, combination or competition? Is it better to divide the spoil or quarrel over it? If the latter alternative be accepted the contest will be a long one and the result uncertain, the successful competitor having moreover the prospect before him that he may have the same battle to fight over again with some new rival at some future time. If the former, competitors have only to fix prices to suit themselves and all will go smoothly, their capital safe, and their future profits secure. The London gas companies furnish an illustration of the working of this kind of combination. Each new company on starting claimed the support of the public, on the ground that competition was beneficial to them, and each commenced by making a reduction in the price of gas. But the reduction in every instance was only a temporary one, for no sooner had a company got beyond the preliminary stage, and established a firm footing, than it combined with the existing institutions to raise the price; and this combination has now, by an arrangement amongst its members, apportioned to each company a particular district within which it has to confine its operations, and is left free to charge whatever price it likes to consumers. Thus, instead of there being only one monopoly for all London, there is a separate monopoly in every district where a company exists, so that consumers are actually worse off now than they were before, as they have to maintain some seven or eight establishments instead of one, each of which has its separate staff of officers, buildings, mains, and capital on which interest has to be paid, all of which must ultimately come out of the pockets of consumers.

Wholesale and retail houses.

Business firms with immense capital adopt another method of neutralizing competition. They give large credit. They induce their customers to trade beyond their capital, and having once got them in their power, they compel them to take their goods at their own prices. This is the kind of relationship that exists between the wholesale mercantile firms in London and the shopkeepers in the provinces, between the millers and the bakers, and between the brewers and the publicans. These wholesale dealers have what they call their clients, people who are under monetary obligation to them. One or two of the great London brewers, for example, have nearly the whole of the metropolitan publicans in their power, each brewer having his own retail houses, which he furnishes and stocks with liquor. Competition on the part of the publican is, under such circumstances, out of the question. The publicans are simply employés of the brewers. They cannot purchase their liquors where they are best or cheapest, but must take them from the brewer who is their landlord and creditor, who accordingly charges very much what he likes for what he supplies them.

Small manufacturers and wholesale houses.

The small manufacturers, who are endeavouring to carry on business with insufficient capital, are subjected to the same kind of fleecing process as the retail dealers. In times of depression they have to depend on the wholesale houses with which they deal for assistance to meet their financial engagements. "One who has thus committed himself," says Mr. Herbert Spencer, "has either to sell his accumulated stock at a sacrifice—30 or 40 per cent. below its value—or else mortgage it; and when the wholesale house becomes the mortgagee, the manufacturer has little chance of escape. He is obliged to work at the wholesale dealer's terms; and ruin almost immediately follows. As was said to us," he adds, "by one of the larger silk hosiers, who had watched the destruction of many of his smaller brethren, 'they may be spared for a time, as a cat spares a mouse, but they are sure to be eaten up in the end.'"[1] Observation of the course pursued in these and similar cases seems to have had some effect on Mill, who by no means goes so far as his followers in praise of competition. Indeed, he is careful to specially caution his readers about attaching too much importance to this principle. After pointing out that the division of produce is the result of two determining agencies, competition and custom, he says:

[1] *Essays, Scientific, Political, and Speculative,* vol. ii. pp. 114, 115.

"Political economists generally, and English political economists above others, have been accustomed to lay almost exclusive stress upon the first of these agencies, (namely, competition); to exaggerate the effects of competition, and to take little account of the other and conflicting principle. . . . But it would a great misconception of the actual course of affairs, to suppose that competition exercises in fact this unlimited sway."[1] And in his evidence before a select committee of the House of Commons, he makes the admission, that consumers would probably be benefited if nine-tenths of the whole of the retail dealers of the country were altogether dispensed with.[2]

Sale by auction.

Nothing in the shape of competition could be fairer, one would imagine, than open sale by auction. But even here capital carries everything before it. The *bonâ-fide* purchaser, the man who wants an article for use, and who is willing to give a fair price for it, can seldom obtain it without first paying black-mail to the speculative capitalist who intrudes himself between the intending buyer and the seller. So badly has the auction system worked in the Australian colonies that, one by one, they have abandoned it in the disposal of their public lands. There could be no possibility of

[1] *Principles*, vol. i. book ii. ch. iv. 1.

[2] June 6th, 1850. His words are:—"If the business of distribution, which now employs, taking the different classes of dealers and their families, perhaps more than a million of inhabitants of this country, could be done by a hundred thousand people, I think the nine hundred and ninety nine thousand might be dispensed with."

fraud or favour in open competition, it was argued, and it was the best mode of securing the highest price for the public estate. And it did certainly seem plausible enough to infer that the man who would give the highest price for a thing would turn it to the best account. The result proved very different, however. The speculative capitalist did not turn the land to the best account, or to any account at all, for he simply held it till he found a purchaser at a price in advance of what he had paid for it; and the intending seller, or the man who would have turned it to the best account, could only obtain what he wanted by paying the capitalist to retire from the contest, or by repurchasing it from him after the sale at an advanced price. All that the capitalist had to do in order to bring about this result, was to occasionally, and by way of example, run up a lot to such a figure as to show the poor man that a successful contest with a rich man was absolutely hopeless.

New South Wales land sales.

As a result of this experience, nearly all the Australian colonies have, as I have said, abandoned the system of sale by auction, and now dispose of the public estate by free selection at a fixed price, and by what is called deferred payments, that is, payments to be extended over a lengthened period. In New South Wales, however, both systems are in full operation, and large quantities of land are still disposed of by auction in that colony, but with results that cannot be considered satisfactory from a public point of view. Sale by auction, in fact, has degenerated into an organized system of fraud. Owing to the high price of wool of late years, the squatters or sheep-farmers in that colony, who graze their immense flocks on public lands at a merely nominal charge, have become wealthy, and many of them have, by this system of sale, been able to purchase the fee simple of large portions of their holdings at the upset price of 20*s.* an acre. And they managed it in this way. They formed themselves into a society called "The Riverine Defence Association," which has large funds at its disposal, for the sole purpose of recouping the occupier of any holding, who is a member of the Association, any sum he might have to pay for the land over and above the upset price, the understanding being that, in case of competition, the price should be run up to any amount rather than allow any intruder to obtain the smallest portion of it. The result of this combination has been what was anticipated, for, after two or three attempts at competition on the part of the public, the organization can now rely on getting every acre of land at the upset price.

National competition.

That the tendency of competition is towards monopoly is as true of nations as it is of individuals or corporations. Some countries impose prohibitive customs duties on imports, for the avowed purpose of excluding outside competition and securing for their own manufacturers the whole of the home trade. Some even go so far as to offer bounties on exports, for the purpose of securing the foreign as well as the home trade, as France, for instance, has done in the matter of beet sugar. Even England, notwithstanding her free-trade proclivities, indirectly does all that she can to prevent any real competition with her on the part of other countries, and to this end her immense resources are used with crushing effect. At present she practically enjoys a monopoly of many lucrative branches of manufacture. With her natural advantages in coal and iron, with her acquired advantages of being the first in the field, and of having a numerous body of well-trained artisans, and, above all, of the immense capital at her disposal, she would be able to maintain her manufacturing supremacy as long as the rate of wages is not materially increased. Her only danger lies in this direction. "Dear labour," says Mr. Brassey, "is the greatest obstacle to the extension of British trade."[1] Hence the extreme solicitude displayed by the trading classes of England at the present day on the question of wages; hence also the growing antagonism which has sprung up of late years between them and the wages-earning class. The manner in which English capital is used to maintain England's manufacturing supremacy is well understood abroad. In any quarter of the globe where a competitor shows himself who is likely to interfere with her monopoly, immediately the capital of her manufacturers is massed in that particular quarter, and goods are exported in large quantities, and sold at such prices, that outside competition is effectually crushed out. English manufacturers have been known to export goods to a distant market, and sell

---

[1] *Work and Wages*, p. 142.

them under cost price for years, with a view to getting the market into their own hands again. The *modus operandi* is incidentally explained with much *naïveté* in a report published some years ago by order of the House of Commons. "The labouring classes generally," writes Mr. Tremenheere, "in the manufacturing districts of this country, and especially in the iron and coal districts, are very little aware of the extent to which they are often indebted for their being employed at all to the immense losses which their employers voluntarily incur in bad times, in order to destroy foreign competition, and to gain and keep possession of foreign markets. Authentic instances are well known of employers having in such times carried on their works at a loss, amounting in the aggregate to three or four hundred thousand pounds in the course of three or four years. If the efforts of those who encourage the combinations to restrict the amount of labour, and to produce strikes, were to be successful for any length of time, the great accumulations of capital could not then be made, which enable a few of the most wealthy capitalists to overwhelm all foreign competition in times of great depression, and thus to clear the way for the whole trade to step in when prices revive, and to carry on a great business before foreign capital can again accumulate to such an extent as to be able to establish a competition in prices with any chance of success. The large capitals of this country are the great instruments of warfare (if the expression may be allowed) against the competing capital of foreign countries, and are the most essential instruments now remaining, by which our manufacturing supremacy can be maintained."[1] That, I have no doubt, is a very fair, as it is certainly a very candid, statement, of the manner in which English capital is used to crush out foreign competition.

England and her dependencies.

England's commercial policy is, and always has been, the extension of this manufacturing monopoly. It was once proposed in the House of Commons that every American horse should be sent to England to get shod. The spirit that actuated the proposer of this scheme still animates the mother-country in all her dealings with her dependencies. Nothing will satisfy her but a monopoly of the most valuable portion of their trade. Mr. Froude has told us how England governed Ireland in her own interests; how she destroyed the Irish woollen manufactures, the export of farm produce and salted provisions, and for a time repressed and curtailed the Irish linen trade. We know how she lost her American colonies, and it is very certain she would have lost several more of her dependencies had she not permitted them the management of their own affairs.

The Indian cotton duties.

It may be thought that all this is now changed, and that England has long since given up coercing her dependencies for her own commercial advantage. This is quite a mistake. We have only to look at what took place in India the other day

[1] *Report of the Commission appointed to examine into the State of the Population of the Mining Districts*, 1854, quoted by Carey, *Social Science*, vol. i. ch. xvii. 4.

with regard to the cotton duties, to be made aware of the magnitude of such an error. For many years past the Indian tariff imposed a duty of from 3 to 5 per cent. on all cotton goods imported into that country, but raw cotton was admitted duty free. It is to Mr. James Wilson, the great anti-corn-law writer, that India is indebted for this duty, who, curiously enough, after doing his best to induce England to abandon customs duties at home, was the first to recommend their adoption abroad. And the tariff which he introduced worked exceedingly well. The duty on manufactured cottons, in particular, answered every requirement of a tax. It was universal and equitable in its incidence, as all classes, rich and poor alike, used the commodity taxed; and as it was an *ad valorem* duty, it fell on each person according to his wealth. As a tax it was inappreciable; it was not obnoxious in its mode of collection; and, above all, it brought in a large revenue. But in the course of time, when the natives had become dissatisfied with the quality of the calicoes which Lancashire supplied them, this duty, which was imposed for revenue purposes only, acted incidentally as a protection to the local mills which have recently been established there and whose products now come into competition with the British exports. Not a word was uttered against this duty so long as Lancashire continued to enjoy a monopoly of the Indian market; but no sooner was this threatened than Lancashire all at once became concerned about the poor ryot. He was paying too much for his calico, forsooth. If that 5 per cent. import duty were taken off, the Lancashire mill-owners solemnly assured the Secretary for India that the poor ryot should get the full benefit of it. This iniquitous impost was crushing the very life out of him. One deputation expressed themselves as greatly concerned about the land revenue of India, lest it should be diminished in consequence of so many of the natives devoting themselves to agriculture. There was nothing for it, Lancashire said, but the abandonment of the cotton duty. And the Secretary for India quite acquiesced. It was a most impolitic duty, he said, and he promised that it should be taken off as soon as possible; but unfortunately it was not possible to do so just at present, as it brought in something like a million sterling a year to the treasury. Anything, however, that the government could do short of this, should be done to encourage England's most important industry.

The Secretary for India was as good as his word. True, he did not take off the tax on manufactured cottons, but he did the next best thing for Manchester—he imposed a tax on the Indian mill-owners. When the new Indian tariff of 1875 appeared, it was found that the duties on manufactured cottons were only slightly reduced, but that a new and altogether unlooked-for tax of 5 per cent. was imposed on raw cotton imported into India. Every one asked what could be the meaning of this new tax, seeing the public, so far as they had been taken into the confidence of the government, had been asked to consider only what duties it would be advisable to remove. The explanation was not far to seek. It appears that the local mill-owners could not compete with England, even in the Indian market, unless they used along with the short-stapled native, a long-stapled imported, cotton. A tax of 5 per cent. on the long-stapled imported cotton would, therefore, effectually handicap the local manufacturers, and to that extent would act as a protection to the Lancashire mill-owners. The most extraordinary part of the matter was the secrecy and bad faith of the Indian government throughout the whole affair. A pretence was made of consulting the mercantile classes in India with regard to the alterations proposed, and the opinions of the Chambers of Commerce, both at Calcutta and Bombay, were asked and given; but from first to last, the idea of imposing a tax on raw cotton, or any new tax whatever, was never mooted by the government, and never dreamed of by any section of the community in India. The question of the abolition of the duty on manufactured cottons was fully discussed, and public opinion was pretty equally divided on the subject. The people of India were therefore quite as much surprised at this new impost as were the local manufacturers; but when its true meaning was understood, surprise was turned into indignation, and the journals that had heretofore been its staunchest supporters became the bitterest in their condemnation of the course adopted by the government. It was felt on all hands that the conduct of the government in this matter was perfectly indefensible, and that nothing but the most abject subserviency to Manchester could have dictated such a policy. It was openly stated that this duty was imposed solely with a view to injure the Indian manufacturers, and preserve for Manchester a continuance of the monopoly; it was characterised as a wicked device of an alien, despotic, or ignorant government, and the Bombay Chamber of Commerce, and other public bodies in India, publicly protested against it as an unjust and impolitic restriction on the manufactures of India, and contrary to that sound principle of the commercial policy of England, and of other enlightened nations, which requires the state to give every encouragement to the free importation of the raw materials necessary for the development and extension of native manufactures.[1]

---

[1] The Calcutta *Englishman* of August 5th, 1875, said:—"If the details given in the telegram which we publish this morning are correct, the new Tariff Bill is about as infamous a measure as ever a subservient Legislature sought to impose upon a voiceless people. An import duty on raw material is, under any circumstances, one of the worst modes of raising the revenue that can be devised. But the duty which the government is about to impose on a particular quality of raw cotton, imported into this country, is nicely calculated to produce the greatest amount of injury that could possibly be inflicted by such an impost. The present Viceroy is too acute an economist not to know what the effect of such a measure must be; and it is impossible to resist the conviction that it is for the sake of the injury it will inflict on India, that the measure is proposed. The Manchester men have been sharp enough to foresee that they would lose more than they gained by a reduction of the duty on coarse goods, unless measures were at the same time taken to prevent the Indian mills from shifting their competition to the finer classes. The Government of India, too, no doubt foresaw that

The absence of all moral principle on the part of a competitor is the second condition of success. If the chief, or, as the deductionists maintain, the sole end of competition is the ob-

The second condition of success.

---

if they went on abolishing the import duty on one class of cotton goods after another, this item of revenue must gradually be extinguished. They have therefore hit upon a device as effectual as it is wicked—we can apply no milder term to it;—a device which will at once increase their revenue and protect the Manchester manufacturer. They have put a prohibitive duty on the raw material necessary to enable the Indian mills to spin the finer counts of yarn and weave the finer makes of cloths, and thus secure to Manchester a continuance of her present monopoly of these classes of goods. None but an alien government, or a despotic and ignorant government bent on filling its coffers for the nonce at any cost, would have adopted such a course as this. No free people would have thus drawn the knife across their own throats. In the shadow of this enormity, the proposition to recoup the revenue for the reduction of duties which fall on the community at large, by raising those which fall chiefly on a section of them already heavily taxed, appears so small as scarcely to justify complaint. As to the merits of the Bill, they are so completely eclipsed by its iniquity, that they cease to invite comment."

The *Bombay Gazette*, which, up to this time, had been a warm supporter of the government proposals, said, on the 10th of August:—"The only subject of regret connected with the new Tariff is, that the reasons which Lord Northbrook undoubtedly could give for putting a duty of 5 per cent. on long-stapled cotton are not generally known. That duty is a new feature in the Customs Tariff for which no one outside the Viceroy's Council was prepared, and is a very objectionable imposition, but we should probably be charging Lord Northbrook falsely if we imputed to his Lordship, as the *Englishman* does, a secret object of desiring to inflict an injury on India in this way. What the motives were which induced Lord Northbrook to make this extraordinary imposition we cannot, of course, say, but he must have perceived that it would be impossible for any importation of the long-stapled cotton to be made under a 5 per cent. duty by manufacturers in India, and that, therefore, they would be so heavily weighted that competition with Manchester would be useless; in other words, he would be assisting Manchester by tainment of the maximum of wealth with the minimum of expenditure, it is not likely that a competitor will

---

protective duties, a policy she could never dare to adopt herself. Look at the matter whichever way we may, we can only account for this false move that Lord Northbrook has made by supposing him to have been under the influence of a specially evil genius in thus marring the otherwise excellent changes he has made in the Customs Tariff; and we are glad to know that the Bombay Chamber of Commerce has already taken steps to protest publicly against the imposition of the new protective duty."

The memorial of the Bombay Chamber of Commerce to the Viceroy, Lord Northbrook, is an able document, and puts the case on behalf of India with great force. It sets forth—

"That such a duty is contrary to sound principle and good policy, being imposed in restraint of the manufactures of India, and injurious to the general interests of the country.

"That it is wholly without precedent in the commercial history of any enlightened country, and has avowedly been adopted 'in order to place the Indian manufacturer upon the same footing as the importer of piece-goods and yarns.'

"A duty imposed, in the interests of the English manufactures, for the purposes only of prohibiting the people of India from extending and improving their own manufactures, is a measure which, in the existing state of the native industry, is, your Memorialists respectfully submit, unjust and oppressive, and can only result in permanent injury to the country.

"That it brings little or no additional revenue to the State, nor, with the slow progress of Indian manufacture, is there any likelihood of its doing so for many years.

"That the Government of India has again and again promulgated that the duties on imported piece-goods and yarns are levied for revenue purposes only, and not for the protection of any industry. The policy which the English Government, under similar circumstances, adopted, was to replace the sacrifice of the revenue, when Customs duties were abolished in the interest of the consumer by the imposition of direct taxes.

"That there is nothing in the recent commercial system of England, which, either by precedent or analogy, can be held to warrant the imposition of such a duty. Excise duties on manufactures are an be excessively scrupulous as to the means he employs to attain it. As a rule, indeed, the trading classes have

---

exploded doctrine equally with protection. While the free-trade policy of England, on the other hand, by removing all restrictions, gave every encouragement to manufactures, it conferred also great benefits on the country, by giving the people cheaper clothing. But the effect of this duty is to restrain the manufactures, and at the same time, to injure the general interests of the people of India. For, assuming that India could compete successfully with Lancashire in the making of the finer qualities of cloth and yarn, the duty will, by restricting the enterprise and energies of its manufactures, deprive the Indian consumer of the benefit of such competition. Now, the object of all free-trade legislation is the interest of the consumer, and for this object the English Legislature has sanctioned the repeal of protective duties. The repeal of import duties, more especially on articles of such universal use as clothing, confers also like benefits on the consumer; but this requires a healthy competition, which, except among the English manufacturers themselves, does not exist in India in the case of the cotton manufactures now imported, for in these neither India nor any other country has yet been able to compete. But such a measure as a duty levied on the raw material entering into a mauufacture, not with the object of raising revenue, but avowedly to favour a foreign industry, already in the enjoyment of a monopoly, is an anomaly which in England no statesman has ever ventured to bring forward, and which may be productive in this country of the most mischievous consequences.

"That a duty on raw material imported for the purposes of manufacture is opposed to that sound principle of the commercial policy of England and other enlightened nations, which requires the State to give every encouragement to the development and extension of native manufactures.

"That great as are the social and economic benefits which have resulted from the liberal policy of the more enlightened nations of the West, the advantage which India would reap from an extension of its manufactures can hardly be over-estimated. Its entire population is, it is needless to remind your Excellency, dependent on agriculture for its subsistence, and the Government of Bombay has expressed its opinion that no cause has retarded the material progress of most districts of this Presidency so much as the want of a demand for agricultural produce and of an outlet for labour, which the establishment of manufactures is calculated to supply."

been apt learners in the school of the deductionists, more especially in England, where the doctrines of this sect have almost taken the form of a national faith. English manufactured goods at one time had a high reputation all over the world. The fact that they were English was quite guarantee enough that they were well made and of proper materials. And the reputation in which they were held was, on the whole, well deserved. English manufactures were, at the period I refer to, really what they were represented to be; they were made for use, and not for sale merely, as English goods are at the present day. The English workman was taught to do his work honestly and well, and to take a pride in it; the English manufacturer staked his reputation on the quality of the goods which bore his name. This practical honesty, more than anything else, was the cause of England's pre-eminence in manufacturing industry. At the time when her commercial reputation stood highest, the English people showed no toleration of adulteration or fraud in any shape. Fraudulent production of every kind was put down by the strong arm of the law, and the law in this case was but the expression of public opinion. Trade in those days was not considered so much a matter of individual profit as of national honour and prosperity. In the early Acts for the suppression of fraudulent practices in manufacturing of goods (and the adulterations were mild then, compared with what they are now), adulterators were stigmatized as "covetous," as men who "practised falsehood," who had more regard for their own private gains than "the advancement of truth," and their practices generally were characterised as "the shame of the land."[1] The fraudulent manufacturer of those days could not hold up his head in decent society, become an office-bearer in his church, take the chair at social and religious gatherings, or send a member of his firm to represent his borough in parliament. He was regarded as a social outlaw and was punished as such.

Modern trade practices.

All this is now changed. The rugged honesty of the English workman and manufacturer is a thing of the past. The old laws against adulteration have been abolished, and almost the only interference with adulteration on the part of the government of the present day has for its object

[1] Take, for instance, the following preamble to 5 and 6 Edward VI. c. 6., entitled "An Act for the making of Woollen Cloth." "Where heretofore divers and many goodly Statutes have been made for the true making of cloth within this realm, which nevertheless, forasmuch as clothiers, some for lack of knowledge and experience, and some of extreme covetousness, do daily more and more study rather to make many than to make good cloths, having more respect to their private convenience and gain than the advancement of truth and the continuance of the commodity in estimation of the worthness thereof, have and do daily instead of truth, practice falsehood, and instead of substantial making of cloth, do practice slight and slender making . . . to the great slander of the King our Sovereign lord and the shame of the land, and to the utter destruction of so great and notable a commodity as the like is not in any foreign nation; our Sovereign lord and King, therefore minding to advance all truth and abandon falsehood, and also to provide for the continuance of the said commodity of cloth making to his honour and the common profit of the realm, hath, by the advice," etc. See also 3 Hen. VIII. c. 6; 23 Hen. VIII. c. 17; 1 Eliz. c. 12.

the protection of the revenue. The manufacturers of tobacco and the importers of tea, for example, are subject to heavy penalties if they have on their premises any ingredients which might be used for the purposes of adulteration; but this is because these goods pay duty at the custom house, and any ingredient which might be mixed with or substituted for them would, *pro tanto*, be a loss to the revenue. Beer, also, is protected from adulteration, because all the materials of which it is composed, with the exception of hops, are liable to excise duty.[1] There has, it is true, been some legislation recently with regard to adulteration, but the vicious doctrines of the English economical school have taken such a firm hold on the public mind that the law has hitherto been practically inoperative.[2] Indeed, fraudulent practices have become the rule and honest trading the exception in England at the present day. It may be safely affirmed that no

---

[1] Until very recently there was also a duty on hops, but this was repealed some time ago, as it was believed it had the effect of encouraging the brewers to use cheaper and less wholesome substitutes. The effect, however, was the very opposite of what was expected. When the duty was repealed, it was no longer necessary for the protection of the revenue to see that hops were used in the manufacture of beer, and the brewers being thus left to themselves, adopted other and cheaper ingredients as substitutes, and the consumption of hops seriously declined in consequence. To such an extent was this the case, that a deputation representing the hop-growers of England, recently waited upon the Chancellor of the Exchequer, and urged him to reimpose the duty which had been taken off in their interest and at their solicitation.

[2] The following paragraph indicates pretty correctly the state of opinion among the English trading classes on this question:—" At a meeting of

country in the world has such a bad reputation in this respect. It is pre-eminently the land of adulteration. Mr. Herbert Spencer is well known to be opposed to legislative interference with trade in any shape, and his testimony as to the extent to which such practices are now carried in England may be taken as thoroughly impartial. "On all sides," he says, "we have found the result of long personal experience to be the conviction that trade is essentially corrupt. In tones of disgust or discouragement, reprehension or derision, according to their several natures, men in business have one after another expressed or implied this belief. Omitting the highest mercantile classes, a few of the less common trades, and those exceptional cases where an entire command of the market has been

---

grocers, provision-dealers, and publicans, which assembled the other day at Wolverhampton, in response to a letter from the secretary of the 'National Chamber of Trade,' to put pressure on Mr. Villiers, one of the members for that town, who had the audacity a short time ago, in the House of Commons, to express the opinion that adulteration was 'still rampant,' it is noteworthy that the chairman at the meeting strongly objected to the appointment of analysts under the bill being vested in the county magistrates, although, while insisting on its being left with the local authorities, he also advocated the establishment of a court of appeal from the decisions of the local Solons. His notions of what constitutes free-trade, presumably also those of other persons present, appear likewise to be very peculiar. 'Mr. Villiers,' he said, 'was an old free-trader, and he could not imagine what that gentleman was thinking about, unless he was going against the opinions of a large number of his constituents. As a free-trader, he was bound to give freedom to every tradesman, and the course he proposed would be very hard to all tradesmen who were affected by the Food and Drugs Adulteration Bill.'"—*Iron*, July 15th, 1875.

obtained, the uniform testimony of competent judges is, that success is incompatible with strict integrity. To live in the commercial world it appears necessary to adopt its ethical code; neither exceeding nor falling short of it; neither being less honest nor more honest. Those who sink below its standard are expelled, while those who rise above it are pulled down to it or ruined. As, in self-defence, the civilized man becomes savage among savages, so it seems that, in self-defence, the scrupulous trader is obliged to become as little scrupulous as his competitors. It has been said that the law of the animal creation is, 'Eat to be eaten;' and of our trading community it may similarly be said its law is, 'Cheat and be cheated.' A system of keen competition, carried on, as it is, without moral restraint, is very much a system of commercial cannibalism." And further on he adds: "On all sides we have met with the same conviction, that for those engaged in the ordinary trades there are but two courses—either to adopt the practices of their competitors or to give up business. Men in different occupations and in different places; men naturally conscientious, who manifestly chafe under the degradations they submitted to, have one and all expressed to us the sad belief that it is impossible to carry on trade with strict rectitude. Their concurrent opinion, independently given by each, is that the scrupulously honest man must go to the wall."[1]

---

[1] *Essays*, vol. ii. p. 134.

Such is Mr. Herbert Spencer's testimony to the extent of the corruption that exists in commercial circles at the present day. And we have no reason to believe that his views are exaggerated. Fraud in one or other of its thousand shapes meets us at every turn in every hour of the day. Everything we buy is different from what it is represented to be, and everything we eat, drink, or wear is adulterated more or less, so that we seem actually to be living in an atmosphere of fraud.

Are openly tolerated and defended.

The worst of it is, that while everybody knows of such practices, nobody seems to be ashamed of them. They are not only tolerated, but in some quarters they are actually defended. For years past the Lancashire mill-owners have been making a kind of calico for the Indian and China markets the material of which consists of about two-thirds cotton and one-third flour sizing and china clay.[1] In the East this kind of cloth goes under the name of mildewed cotton, owing to the fact that goods so manufactured generally arrived at their destination in a mildewed condition. On this account the merchants to whom these goods are consigned have long and loudly protested against this system of adulteration. But they also objected on another account. It appears that the natives of

[1] At a meeting of the representatives of the various Operatives' Associations of Lancashire, Cheshire, and Derbyshire, held at Blackburn, on the 25th July last, it was stated, and I have yet seen no contradiction of the statement on the part of the manufacturers, that calicoes were now adulterated to the extent of from 80 to 90 per cent.—See *Manchester Examiner and Times*, July 26th, 1876.

those countries object to buy paste and china clay at the price of good cloth, and that the exports of Lancashire calicoes are likely to be seriously diminished if this system is not put an end to. The Chambers of Commerce at Shanghai and other places have accordingly remonstrated strongly with the Manchester Chamber of Commerce on the matter (an appeal to the government being out of the question in these days), and the subject came formally before the latter body last year,[1] when, after a full discussion, the Chamber came to the conclusion that any interference with the present practices was not desirable.

Man-chester Chamber of Commerce.

Still more recently the Bombay Chamber of Commerce refused to sanction the putting down of adulteration. The dissatisfaction of the natives of India with the adulterated calicoes of Lancashire has helped, along with other causes, to re-establish the manufacture of cotton in India, and a considerable number of mills have recently been erected in the neighbourhood of Bombay and on the banks of the Hooghly, near Calcutta.[2] As several of the Bombay mill-owners had begun to imitate the ways of Manchester in over-sizing their calico, and to prevent, if possible, the ruin that would be certain to result from the general adoption of the system, Mr. Ashburner, the

The Bombay Chamber of Commerce.

[1] 1875.

[2] The *Times of India* says: "The local mill industry owes its success mainly to the disatisfaction of the purchasers of Manchester goods with the dishonest system of mixing with the cotton some 30 per cent. of China clay."

Revenue Commissioner for the Northern Division of the Bombay Presidency, urged, in a letter to the government, that an Act for the prevention of frauds in the preparation of cloth in the Bombay mills should be passed, as it was probable that if once the mill-owners became accustomed to derive large profits from adulteration it would be extremely difficult to stop the practice afterwards. The question was referred to the Bombay Chamber of Commerce, a body which is chiefly composed of English merchants and the agents of English firms, and in a lengthy document they endeavoured to show that any interference of the legislature with "the course of trade" was unnecessary and pernicious.[1]

How such evils right themselves.

I may be told that these evils will right themselves in time; that the frauds will be discovered, and that people will then refuse to have any dealings with those who perpetrate them. But human ingenuity is not easily exhausted. No sooner is one kind of fraud discovered and put down than another

[1] Mr. Ashburner replied to the objections of the Bombay Chamber of Commerce, in a letter to the Government, in which he says:— "I was fully prepared for the opposition of the Chamber of Commerce. The Chamber is composed of gentlemen whose interest in this country is limited to a few years' residence; their business is to buy and sell; and any interference with their operations, however necessary for the welfare of the country, is, of course, highly prejudicial to their interests. A bale of adulterated cloth is as much an article of trade as one that is honestly prepared. There is a large demand for such cloth; their business is to supply the demand; and they naturally object to the interference of Government, and quote Mill and the 'Economists' to prove that any interference of the Legislature with trade is unnecessary and pernicious."

immediately crops up in its place, so that the prospect of things righting themselves in this way is distant enough, and meanwhile the public suffer. But how do such evils right themselves? Only by the ruin of the trade of the country which tolerates them. The mill-owners of Lancashire are doing their best to ruin their own trade, as the flourishing condition of the numerous cotton mills in India at the present moment testify.[1]

One cause of high customs tariffs.

The speechmakers of the Cobden Club declaim loudly enough against high customs tariffs, but they ought to know that the dishonesty of English manufacturers has a good deal to do with some of these tariffs at all events. It is well known that

---

[1] Not only has her India and China trade already been seriously injured, as is proved by the decrease in the exports, but even her home trade is threatened. The *Warehousemen and Drapers' Journal* for October, 1875, announced that it had just received the startling intelligence that Manchester is importing calicoes and long-cloths of American manufacture, and adds:—"For some time past it has been known that American ladies travelling in Europe uniformly refuse to purchase cotton goods made on this side of the Atlantic, and send to their own country for supplies. Messrs. Wanklyn, O'Hanlon and Co., of Manchester, thought it important to inquire the reason; they found the American fabrics much better in quality and appearance than the European manufacture, and the first shipment that has ever been made in the ordinary course of business to this country has just reached them. Is protectionist America really to distance free-trade England in an industry so peculiarly her own, and in which she has hitherto considered herself beyond rivalry? If the warning needs to be intensified, we can add another fact scarcely less significant—that one of the largest houses in the city has been for some time past importing calicoes from Belgium." Since the above was written American calicoes have been extensively introduced into England and Australia, where they command a ready sale, being found to be both better and cheaper than the English-made article.

the United States had at one time a large and profitable trade with the West Indian colonies and the South American States.[1] She supplied these countries with numerous manufactures of her own, and especially with a kind of cotton fabric suited to the climate. A cheap imitation of this cloth was made in Lancashire, and exported in such quantities to these countries, that the sound American article was completely driven out of the market. In the East, the United States had also a large export trade, but she was cut out by the same dishonest practices. Need we wonder that, finding their foreign trade gone, the Americans began to think it time to secure their home trade by the imposition of high customs duties?

Case of Victoria.

In adopting this course the United States did what a British colony has more recently been compelled to do under precisely similar circumstances. A cloth factory was established in Victoria some years ago, and doing a fair business, the company that owned it paying a dividend of about 10 per cent. on the amount of capital invested. A superior kind of tweed was made at this mill, which had a high reputation in the colony owing to its good wearing qualities. But an enterprising Yorkshire manufacturer procured a sample of the cloth, and made a shoddy imitation of it, shipped large quantities of this spurious manufacture to Melbourne, and passed it off for a time

[1] See *The Report of the Select Committee of the House of Commons on Imports*, 1840, questions 1672–1674, and 2000–2005.

as the genuine article, selling it, of course, at a much lower price, so that the locally made article, which was really the cheaper of the two, taking the quality into consideration, became a drug in the market. Up to this time there was no import duty on cloth, but in order to save a promising industry from ruin, and to put a stop to the importation of the fraudulent article, the local Legislature in 1871 imposed a duty of 10 per cent. on all cloth imported into the colony. The consequence of this step has been that, instead of there being only one cloth mill in Victoria, there are now a dozen of them, and new ones are going up all over the country.

Quality of British exports.

British manufacturers have become so accustomed to make goods merely for sale, that they seem almost to have forgotten that they are wanted for use. This is more especially the case when the goods are intended for export. Any rubbish which is quite unsaleable at home is considered quite good enough to send abroad. So long as it is off their hands and the money obtained for it, what is it to them if the article when it arrives at its destination proves to be utterly worthless for the purpose for which it was ordered? Not the least annoying part of the matter is that, when goods come from a distance, the purchaser has often to pay, in the shape of freight, commission, insurance, and other charges, what sometimes amounts to as much as the original price of the goods at the port of departure, so that the importer not only has a useless article thrown on his hands, but is at the same time saddled with heavy charges for its conveyance. Is it extraordinary that under such circumstances consumers sometimes prefer a locally made article to an imported one, which, even if nominally cheap in the first instance, is almost sure to be dearer in the end; and that they are sometimes willing to submit to high customs duties in the hope of some day being able to establish honest manufactures of their own? Three cases of the kind alluded to were recently discovered in three different Australian colonies within a few days of each other. Machinery had been ordered from England by the government of Victoria for pumping out a large graving-dock which, on its arrival, was found to be contrary to specification, and quite unfit for the purpose for which it was ordered, and the necessary alterations, which had to be made in the colony at great cost and inconvenience, amounted to as much as the original cost of the whole. About the same time the government of New Zealand received from England a shipment of iron rails, being a portion of an order for 160 miles of railway, which, on examination, proved to have been made of cinder with only a coating of iron outside. Within the same week a first portion of another consignment of iron rails, for some hundreds of miles of railway, arrived in Sydney for the government of New South Wales, which, on being tested, turned out to be of a quality similar to that sent to New Zealand. These materials, be it observed, were in each case made by "highly respectable" firms, and though every precaution had been taken by the respective governments to have them properly examined before shipment, the result was as I have stated. If governments are served in this fashion, how are private individuals likely to fare? Some day or other England will wake up and find herself without a character and without an export trade.

No doubt evils of this sort will right themselves in the end, but at what cost? If the loss fell exclusively on the dishonest trader it would not matter much, but unfortunately he is about the last one that feels it. It is the country which tolerates his existence that usually suffers all the loss. And the evils, if allowed to work their own remedy, will only do so at the expense of the country's honour and the country's trade. When there are no longer any customers to cheat, cheating will no doubt be abandoned as an unprofitable business, just as the thieves' occupation will be gone when there is nothing to steal. But why the fate of the thief should be so different from that of the dishonest trader, who flourishes on his gains in all the odour of respectability, is one of the mysteries which the economists have left unexplained. They both take what does not belong to them; they both bring discredit on the country; but, if anything, the dishonest trader is worse than the thief, for, in addition to all this, he helps to ruin the country which supports him.

In the early history of the human race the maxim of the economists was in full force. It was then each man for himself. There was no interchange of ideas between man and man, no reciprocity of sentiments, no mutual dependence. All the elements which composed society were in a state of repulsion. To be a man was to be a competitor for the limited means of subsistence, and therefore an enemy. Socially, we have since changed all that. There are now recognized rights, and acknowledged obligations with respect to them, and modern society is the result. Can it be said that we have made as much progress industrially? Is not the struggle for industrial existence as keen, as unscrupulous, and as deadly as ever it was? Do not competitors regard each other as enemies, who are to be got rid of at all hazards and as soon as possible? Why, may I ask, should the static condition of the industrial world be one of warfare? Why should the man of large capital be allowed to crush his weaker rival, or the honest trader be ruined by the rogue? Why, in fact, should not industry be conducted on the principles of justice, instead of, as at present, by brute force and cunning?

Industrial progress does not keep pace with social.

I may be told that competition is a law of nature, and that the struggle for existence is as fierce and unrelenting in the animal as it is in the economic world. This is undoubtedly true; but there is this material difference between the two cases. Economists insist (I speak of the English school, of course), that competition is the proper thing under all circumstances and allow no exception to this rule. But nature is more just. Nature provides that those only shall compete who are fitted for the struggle. Parental instincts protect the young from the competition to which the parents readily expose themselves; while among animals of the same species opposite sexes do not compete with each other. The struggle for existence is only for the strong, the full grown, and fully trained of the same sex. But it is not so in the economic world. There it is the stronger against the weaker sex, the full-grown man against the infant; and when a man is down it is considered the proper thing to kick him and jump upon him.

Political Economy and Morals.

But I shall probably be told that Political Economy has nothing to do with Morals. I am aware that Political Economy is usually considered as belonging to an entirely different department of scientific investigation, and that when an action comes to be regarded in its moral aspect, it is supposed to pass out of the region of Economic Science into that of Ethics. But this position is altogether untenable. Wherever there are two individuals (and there always must be whenever an act of exchange takes place) there must necessarily be two separate and antagonistic interests to be adjusted. What is fraud but an exclusive regard by an individual to his own interest, or, what is the same thing, a disregard of the interests of others? An act does not cease to be an industrial or economic act because it is an unjust or immoral one. It does not thereby pass out of the region of Political Economy into Ethics, but it belongs equally to both departments at one and the same time. It is still the same act whether regarded in its economic or its moral aspect. We might as well say that when an immoral act is committed which renders the agent amenable to the criminal law, that the act thereby passes out of the moral sphere into that of the social or political. But the act still remains an immoral, while at the same time it is a criminal act, although it may now be called a misdemeanour or a felony, and be taken cognisance of by the civil authorities.

Economists subordinate social to individual interests.

Among the ancient writers the tendency had been to subordinate the individual to society, individual interests to social interests. Human nature was judged of by the mass, and the individual was ignored. The deductionists have adopted the converse method, and subordinate society to the individual. But, as we have already pointed out, they have failed to take into account some important elements of man's nature. Having committed this error it was natural that they should commit another and ignore individual relationships altogether. And this is what they have actually done. They have proceeded on the assumption that there is but one individual in the whole world, and that any act of his affects only himself, and has no relation to any body else. Under such circumstances there could, of course, be no relationship to adjust, and the moral element would thus be effectually got rid of.

The moral element cannot be disposed of so easily,

however, for it is inherent in every human action, and must necessarily be recognized in every relation of life.

The moral element essential.

It is the force that gives cohesion to the social organism. Without it there could be no division of labour, no exchange of products, no social intercourse. Society could have no existence if there were no rights and no corresponding duties. Even domestic life would be unbearable if the principles of justice were disregarded between husband and wife, and between parents and children. The moral element is even necessary in our pleasures. Our very pastimes require to be conducted on the principles of fair play. What, for example, would become of our national sport if jockeys were got at, if false weights or unjust scales were used, if horses were doctored, and their owners paid to lose the race? Such practices are not altogether unknown on the turf at present, but what would be the result if, instead of being the exception, they became the rule, and were condoned and defended by the highest authorities in such matters? How much more necessary, then, is the moral element in our industrial relations when every contract between buyer and seller, between producer and consumer, between debtor and creditor, and between master and servant, is based on the truthfulness and fidelity of each of the contracting parties?

PART II.

PRINCIPLES.

CHAPTER VI.

INDUSTRIAL FORCES.

Adam Smith's premisses in his *Wealth of Nations.*

In his *Wealth of Nations*, Adam Smith assumes as the cause of industrial phenomena "the desire of every man to better his condition." This desire he describes as "constant, uniform, and universal," which "comes to us from the womb, and never leaves us till we go into the grave," and this, and this alone, he maintains, is sufficient to carry society to wealth and prosperity. Throughout his work he keeps this motive constantly in view, and from it, as cause, he traces all the phenomena of industrial life. He nowhere states that man, in the pursuit of wealth, is not influenced by other motives, but this is implied throughout.

And in his *Moral Sentiments.*

In his *Moral Sentiments*, on the other hand, where he had phenomena of a totally different kind to explain, Adam Smith has recourse to totally different premisses. Man is no longer selfish but sympathetic; and sympathy he describes as something essentially different from selfishness. "Sympathy," he remarks, "cannot in any sense be regarded as a selfish principle."[1] "The desire to better one's condition" henceforth takes a subordinate place in his system. There is another principle which should determine every act, and this is the principle of justice. "There is one virtue," he says, "which the general rules determine, with the greatest exactness, every external action which it requires. This virtue is justice. The rules of justice are accurate in the highest degree, and admit of no exceptions or modifications but such as may be ascertained as accurately as the rules themselves, and which generally, indeed, flow from the very same principles with them. If I owe a man ten pounds, justice requires that I should pay him precisely ten pounds, either at the time agreed on, or when he demands it. What I ought to perform, how much I ought to perform, when and where I ought to perform it, the whole nature and circumstances of the action prescribed, are all of them precisely fixed and determined."[2] He even goes so far as to trace the desire of wealth to the sympathetic affections, as, he says, "it is chiefly for this regard to the sentiments of mankind that we pursue riches and avoid poverty," and, again, "to become the natural object of the joyous congratulations and sympathetic attentions of mankind, are the circumstances which give to prosperity all its dazzling

[1] *Moral Sentiments*, vol. i. p. 206. Bohn's Edition. Compare vol. i. p. 9, where he combats the views of those "who are fond of deducing all our sentiments from certain refinements of self-love."

[2] *Moral Sentiments*, vol. ii. pp. 249, 250.

splendour."[1] There is no possibility of reconciling these two sets of premisses. Man cannot at the same time be wholly selfish and wholly sympathetic. If wholly selfish, then he cannot be sympathetic, and if wholly sympathetic, he cannot be selfish. It is true he may be both selfish and sympathetic, and this is in effect what Adam Smith proves by a roundabout process. But both statements are wrong as he puts them, and the deductions which he draws from them cannot be otherwise than misleading.

Difference between his premisses and those of the deductionists.

Adam Smith's method of a century ago is the method of the deductionists of to-day. They not only treat the subject deductively as he did, but they have adopted substantially the same premisses, the phrase, "desire for wealth," being substituted for "the desire to better one's condition." Viewed from the modern standpoint, man is still purely selfish. No account has been taken of that other class of motives which Adam Smith in his *Moral Sentiments* included under the term Sympathy. No attempt has been made to reconcile the contradictions which are apparent in the premisses of his two great works. If any advantage, in a scientific point of view, could be gained by this process, it would be a different matter; but no one pretends that there is.

In Sociology we do not proceed by separating the social from the anti-social or self-regarding forces.

---

[1] *Moral Sentiments*, vol. i. p. 66.

The method in Social Science.

We do not attempt to establish the science on the basis of the social forces alone. On the contrary, we recognize both as essential to the maintenance of social order and progress. In Social Science we view the two kinds of forces from the standpoint of society, and we subordinate the interests of the individual to those of the community if the well-being of the latter requires it. Where the two interests clash, the lesser must give way to the greater, the individual to society. When, on the other hand, there is no clashing, the two may work side by side; as, for instance, a man may follow any pursuit he likes so long as he does no injury to his neighbour.

The method in Ethics.

It is the same with Ethics. The moralist does not ignore either the self-regarding or the social tendencies of man's nature when he treats of the Ethical Sentiment; on the contrary, he fully recognizes both. The moralist, however, takes a wider range of view than either the economist or sociologist. His standpoint is not that of the individual, or of society, but of humanity at large. He treats of human actions in the abstract, irrespective of individuals or nationalities. But so far from ignoring the existence of self-interest and the social affections, he enjoins the exercise of both. To provide for one's self and one's family he regards as a sacred duty. Prudence and temperance are virtues of a high order. The self-regarding tendencies of our nature are, indeed, indispensable, as they form the basis of the social affections and the ethical sentiment. We can only desire for others what we would wish for ourselves. What an individual desires others should do to him is the standard by which his conduct towards others can alone be regulated. The precepts, "Do unto others as ye would others should do unto you," "Love your neighbour as yourself," embody the purest principles of morality, and they are based on the self-regarding principles of man's nature.

The isolation of motives.

In order to ascertain how a man would act under a variety of motives operating concurrently upon him, it is necessary, we are told, to proceed by ascertaining how he would act under each particular motive taken separately.[1] But this would not be sufficient. Analysis must be followed by synthesis. After ascertaining the operation of each motive taken separately, it would be necessary, next, to ascertain what the effect would be if operating together. A cannon ball is projected by the force of gunpowder. From what we know of the laws of motion, we might conclude that the ball would proceed onward through space at an uniform rate of speed, and in a straight line. But this conclusion would be erroneous, for two other forces here come into play; the one, gravity, deflects the ball to the earth's surface; the other, the resistance of the atmosphere, impedes its progress; and the result of this combination of forces is that the ball, after describing a curve, is speedily brought to the earth's surface.

---

[1] *Unsettled Questions*, p. 139.

In the same manner mental forces impede or counteract one another. The desire of wealth, for instance, like the force of the gunpowder, may be the impelling motive, and from what we know of the laws of mind we might arrive at a tolerably correct conclusion as to its operation; but this motive might be counteracted by others, such as sympathy, or the sense of duty, so that an entirely different result would take place from what might have been expected.

Difference between a force and a law.

It is to be noted, however, that the process here recommended—that, namely, of testing the various forces acting concurrently—is precisely that which the deductionists do not adopt. They have hitherto made no attempt to ascertain the action of those other motives that are concerned in the production of the phenomena under investigation. Indeed, they have only partially examined the operation of the one motive they have adopted as the basis of their system. The first step in this direction would be to discover what those other motives really were, and afterwards their mode of operation. But this field of inquiry the deductionists have left entirely unexplored. They have discovered the existence of one motive, the desire of wealth, and they have not attempted to look for any others. As, however, they admit the existence of other motives, they should ascertain what they are, and next their mode of operation, separately and concurrently. It is absurd to discuss the laws of a science before we have ascertained its forces. The law of gravitation is that it varies directly as the mass, and inversely as the square of the distance; but the existence of gravitation as a force was known before the law was discovered. A law is the mode in which a force operates, and not the force itself, and we can have no knowledge of industrial law till we have first ascertained the forces which produce industrial phenomena.

Different kinds of forces.

A man obtains an income of, let us say, £2000 a year from business, which is all he can possibly earn, and he spends the whole of it on himself. Another man obtains £3000 a year, which is all he can possibly earn, but he spends half of it in charity. A third, who conducts his business on the strictest principles of honesty, obtains only £1000 a year, when, were he less scrupulous, he might as easily earn twice the amount. In each of these cases the impelling motive is undoubtedly the desire of wealth. In the first, we may assume, for argument's sake, this desire to be the sole motive; in the second, however, as one half of the amount earned was spent in charity, we must assume that social sympathy had something to do with the result; in other words, that the desire of wealth was strengthened by the social affections; but in the third, another force comes into operation which does not strengthen but impedes the impelling motive. This is the ethical sentiment. Or take another illustration. A workman is engaged by the week or month at a fixed rate of wages. If his sole motive were the desire to obtain the maximum of wealth by the minimum expenditure of labour, he will do exactly the amount of work, and no more, which will secure him continued employment. Another man, engaged in the same way, and at the same fixed rate of wages, is also impelled by the same motive, but, in addition, has a desire to please his employer, which he thinks he can best do by performing a satisfactory amount of work. The additional motive makes him more energetic, and he works all the better for it. A third man, similarly engaged, is not of a social disposition and has no wish to please anybody in particular, but has a desire to do his duty, and this additional motive induces him to work harder or better than he would otherwise do if his sole motive were a desire to obtain his wages. Here we have two forces, or motives, which the deductionist takes no account of, but which, nevertheless, have undoubted influence on industrial activity.

Motives or impulses are called forces because they move or impel to action. This they do by operating on volition. A motive, however, is only one of a whole series of forces terminating in activity. There is, first, sensation, then emotion, next motive, and, last of all, volition. The muscular sensations are the primary sensibilities; the emotions are secondary, derived, or compound feelings; the sensations or emotions, when viewed in connection with an object as their cause, become motives; and volition is the connecting link between these and the resultant action.

Classification of forces.

Every motive concerned in industrial action may be termed an industrial force. By industrial force I understand that kind of force which produces industrial action; and by industrial action I mean that kind of action which has reference to the production or exchange of wealth, using the latter term in its technical sense. According to the classification usually adopted by ethical writers, motives are of two kinds, Self-regarding and Non-self-regarding, or Egoistic and Altruistic. But we do not ascend from the Egoistic to the Altruistic at a single bound. There is an intermediate stage between the two which must be passed before we can reach the higher. As in inductive science we proceed from a single fact to a series of similar facts before we can arrive at the conception of law; as in language we rise from the concrete through the collective to the abstract; so in Ethics we can reach the Altruistic only through the collective or social stage. Motives may be classified according to the standpoint of the subject of them. As an object, person, or action, for instance, may be viewed from the *I*, *we*, or *other* standpoint, so motives may be viewed and designated according as they refer to one's self only, to others along with one's self, and to others apart from one's self. If regarded from the *I* point of view, or in a strictly personal aspect, motives may be called Egoistic (from ἐγώ); from the *we* point of view, or in a semi-personal or social aspect, they may be called Hemeistic (from ἡμεῖς); and if from *other* than a self-regarding point of view, they may be termed (still preserving the Greek pronominal system of nomenclature) Allostic (from ἄλλος). We apprehend objects, persons, or actions from the first point of view, as it were spontaneously; from the second, with more or less difficulty, according to the extent of our intimacy with those with whom we associate ourselves; and from the third, only by a great mental effort, and after we have been long accustomed to view things from a purely social standpoint. The forces with which we have to deal may therefore be classified as follows:—

I. *The Egoistic,* which have reference to things, and have for their object the gratification of those sensations and emotions which centre in self. They include:—

1. Wants; as food, drink, exercise, rest.
2. Desires; as the comforts, conveniences, and luxuries of life.

II. *The Hemeistic,* which have reference to persons, and have for their object the gratification of the social emotions. They include:—

1. The Affections proper and friendship.
2. The Desires; as admiration, approbation, and esteem of our fellow-men.
3. Motives of the impassioned order; as love, hate, fear, resentment.

III. *The Allostic,* which have reference to actions, and have for their object justice. They include:—

Fidelity, truth, gratitude, generosity, and beneficence.

The Egoistic group I have placed first because it is the strongest, the most important, and because it forms the basis of the two following groups. The Hemeistic I have placed second, because it is inferior in strength and importance to the former, and is superior in both respects to the Allostic. In the order of development, the Egoistic might be designated, to use a geological term, the primary, the Hemeistic the secondary, and the Allostic the tertiary order of industrial forces. The two latter are distinct and independent, but are derivative in their origin, as are motives from emotions, and emotions from sensations.

The relative importance of industrial forces.

The Egoistic forces I have subdivided into (1) Wants and (2) Desires. Among the former I have placed Appetite first, because it is most imperative in its demands, and its influence most conspicuous. To the demands of appetite may be ascribed nearly the whole of the industrial activity we see everywhere around us; and to this, as the remote or proximate cause, may be traced the continual wars among savage tribes, the early migrations of the human race, and the movements of population generally all over the world, past and present. All must eat in order to live, but many live only in order that they may eat. It may indeed be said that the great mass of mankind live for nothing else. Perhaps three-fourths of the human race are content if they can only get enough to satisfy the cravings of appetite,

The first division, or wants.

and provide themselves with decent covering for their bodies. This is more particularly the case in the East, where the great bulk of the population of the globe exists. "The Hindoo workman," says Mr. Brassey, "knows no other want than his daily portion of rice, and the torrid climate renders water-tight habitations and ample clothing unnecessary. The labourer, therefore, desists from work as soon as he has provided for the necessaries of the day. Higher wages would add nothing to his comfort, it only serves to diminish his ordinary industry."[1] Mr. Wallace, the naturalist, speaking of the sago tree as food for the inhabitants of the Malay Archipelago, reckons that one tree will produce food sufficient for one man for a whole year, while two men will prepare it in five days, and two women will take five more days to bake the whole produce into cakes ready for use. "The effect of this cheapness," says Mr. Wallace, "is very prejudicial to the inhabitants of the sago countries, who are never so well off as in those where rice is cultivated. Many of the people have neither vegetables nor fruit, but live almost on sago and a little fish. . . . As far as the comforts of life are concerned they are as much inferior to the wild dyak of Borneo, as to many of the barbarous tribes of the Archipelago."[2] Readers will recall what Humboldt

---

[1] *Work and Wages*, p. 88.

[2] *Malay Archipelago*, vol. i. pp. 121, 122; also pp. 356, 357, where he says that the people of Muka, and Sago Island, live in "that abject state of poverty almost always found where the sago tree is abundant."

says about the effect which the prolific yield of the banana had upon the Indians of Mexico. As long as food was plentiful it was found impossible to make the natives industrious. To have enough to eat was all that they cared for, and when their appetite was satisfied, nothing could move them to the slightest exertion. The cultivation of the potato in Ireland had at one time a similarly injurious effect on the industrial habits of the natives of that country. Speaking of the labouring classes of society in Europe generally, Malthus says, "if the labourer can obtain the full support of himself and family by two or three days' labour; and, if to furnish himself with conveniences and comforts, he must work three or four days more, he will generally think the sacrifice too great compared with the objects to be obtained"[1]—a statement which was strikingly illustrated by the colliers in England and Wales during the coal famine in 1874, when the high wages current at that period enabled them to support themselves by working three days in the week and idling the other three.

The second division, or desires.

In the second subdivision I have placed Desires, or acquired wants. These are not so important as those in the first subdivision. Not being natural, in the sense of being necessary, they are not universal, and vary in strength according to circumstances. Only after they are provided with the

[1] *On Population*, vol. iii. p. 23.

necessaries do mankind begin to think of the conveniences, comforts, and luxuries of life. Desires are stimulated by new objects. The South Sea Islander can usually obtain, by one hour's labour, food enough to support him for twenty-four, but he will work continuously for long periods in order to obtain some article of European manufacture which has taken his fancy. A Fijian has been known to labour for three, and even for six months, in the plantations of European settlers in order to procure a knife, tomahawk, or some other article of trifling value; and no sooner had he obtained this than he would be attracted by some other object and serve a like term in order to procure it. But in this respect the civilized man is little better than the savage, for no sooner has he gratified one desire than he creates another. He is never satisfied with what he has but is always seeking more. Contentment is not one of the virtues of civilization. With all the accumulated experience of the race, with the inherited wealth of centuries, with the discoveries of science, the improvements of labour-saving machines and in the means of locomotion, we do not find that the modern civilized man toils any less, or is more contented than his forefathers. The cheaper an article becomes, the less we esteem it. The more plentiful any material, the more we waste it. A machine is invented that makes twenty stitches for one that could formerly be made by hand, and we now put in twenty stitches for one that we put in formerly. The more we have, the more we spend. Value is not synonymous with utility but with scarceness. As old desires are satisfied, new ones take their places, and in all probability there will never come a time when this will be changed, and that community which has surpassed all others in the creation of artificial wants shall not be deemed the most, but the least civilized. According to Say, that society is most civilized which produces most and consumes most, or, in other words, which has the greatest number of artificial wants.

The Hemeistic forces.

We come now to the second, or Hemeistic group of forces. Man is not made to live alone. His mental, no less than his physical organization, compels him to associate with his fellows. Every one is related to some one else. A man has, or has had, a father and mother; he may have a brother or sister, or some other relatives; and these relationships he cannot divest himself of, or the associations connected with them. But his associations extend beyond the domestic circle and embrace friends, acquaintances, and ultimately society at large; and these associations call forth certain emotions and desires which we designate the social affections. The deductionist, however, accepts only those motives included under the first group in our list, and rejects those included under the second and third. Personal motives only are retained, and social and moral are rejected. Why is this? Is man, in his industrial relations, not influenced by motives of a social character? Is parental, filial, or conjugal affection no incentive to action? Does a man never act for friendship's sake? Does a workman never put forth an effort in order to obtain the approbation of his employer, or the esteem of his fellows? Does an employer never do anything with a view to secure the respect and esteem of his workmen? On the contrary, do we not find that men in every condition of life are continually acting with a view to obtain the good opinion of others, and do they not constantly abstain from acts which, though beneficial to themselves are hurtful to others, for fear of incurring the hatred or contempt of their fellow-creatures? We all know, indeed, that motives of this kind largely influence industrial activity. Why, then, ignore them? The emotions, or motives of the impassioned order, as love, anger, fear, also belong to this group. The deductionist, however, takes no account of them whatever, although they are forces of the very greatest importance in industrial activity. They act on volition, which they strengthen or weaken according to circumstances. If I love a person, I will avoid doing him an injury, and will probably exert myself on his behalf. If I am angry with a person, I will not go out of my way to do him a service; I might even avoid doing something I had previously determined on, because it might be to his advantage; and if he is a rival in business, my feeling towards him will give strength to my resolution to secure success at his expense. Why are all such motives ignored? We grant that they are awkward elements for the deductionist to deal with, but that surely is no reason why we should ignore them. If they cannot be made to fit in with our system, so much the worse for our system.

The Allostic forces.

The last group on the list is the Allostic, which also, though in a lesser degree, is largely concerned with industrial activity. Every man has a certain rule of propriety, or τὸ δέον, according to which he shapes his conduct. This rule or standard we call duty or honour. In acting up to this standard, a man will often do what is contrary to his personal gain, as, for instance, when he pays a just debt that has never been claimed, and is never likely to be; when he corrects an error in his favour in an account which has been presented to him for payment, and which would not otherwise be detected; when he pays for an article more than is asked, because he believes it to be worth it; when he sells a sound article when he could make a larger profit by selling a spurious one; when he pays his creditors in full, after obtaining a legal discharge from his debts. In acting up to this standard he may even do what is contrary to his social instincts, as when he would rather witness the sufferings of those who are bound to him by the ties of affection than be guilty of a dishonourable act, or when he prefers a conscientious discharge of duty to fame, power, or social advancement. In these and all similar cases a man does what he considers to be proper, honourable, or just, and apart altogether from motives appealing to his personal or social interests. It is not necessary we should in this place go into the question of the origin of this standard. Whether it be intuitive or acquired makes no difference. It is enough for our purpose that it exists, and that it is of the character here described.

CHAPTER VII.

ON VALUE.

THE modern school of economists do not approve of the distinction which Adam Smith makes between value in use, and value in exchange. They have only one kind of value, namely, value in exchange. Value, in the language of economists, means, according to Mill, exchange value; and he tells us that when he does not use the adjunct "exchange," it must always be understood.[1] This definition of the word has been generally concurred in by subsequent writers.

Value in use and in exchange.

By value, or exchange value, Mill understands "general purchasing power," or, "the command which its possession gives over purchaseable commodities in general."[2] Senior defines it to be "that quality in a thing which fits it to be given or received in exchange;"[3] and Prof. Cairnes

Various definitions of value.

[1] *Principles*, vol. i. book iii. ch. i. 3.
[2] *Ibid.* vol. i. book iii. ch. i. 2.
[3] *Political Economy*, p. 14.

describes it as "the ratio in which commodities in open market are exchanged against each other."[1] These definitions all agree in expressing the idea of exchangeability. In this view of the meaning of value I am unable to concur.

Exchange-ability not an essential element in value.

Value is no doubt an essential element in exchange, but exchange is not an essential element in value. There is, I conceive, a manifest difference between value in use, and value in exchange, which modern writers have overlooked. Value in use is holders' value; value in exchange is sellers' value. A man may hold a thing, not in order to sell or exchange it, but in order to use it. Many things possess value that are not exchangeable at all. Indeed, if we limit value by things exchangeable, we shall exclude a large and very important class of commodities. A man may possess an article which may be altogether unsaleable, and yet he may place a very high value upon it because he understands its uses and can turn it to a profitable account. A labour-saving machine, for instance, may have no exchange value, as the public may have no faith in its capabilities, or so little confidence in the skill of the inventor that they may not trouble themselves even to inquire about it. The value of the invention may ultimately come to be recognized, but in the first instance, practical men hold aloof and will have nothing to do with it. Again, an

---

[1] *Some Leading Questions*, p. 1.

emigrant may take a plough of modern manufacture to some distant part of the world, say to the East, where the natives have been accustomed to scratch the soil with an implement which dates its origin from the time of the Pharaohs. In such a place the modern plough would find no purchaser; nor would the emigrant gain anything by sending it back from whence it came, as the cost of conveyance might be more than the article would fetch. The plough, therefore, would have no exchange value, because no one would buy it where it was, and if he sent it back to where there were purchasers he would gain nothing by it. But suppose the importer used it himself in cultivating the soil, could it then be said to possess no value to him? On the contrary, would not the very cause that had rendered it valueless in exchange, namely, the distance from a purchaser, make it all the more valuable to him under the circumstances? Or take another case. An enterprising emigrant takes up a section of land in one of the islands of the South Pacific for the purpose of growing cotton for the English market. Suppose that the soil and climate were everything that could be desired, that labour was cheap, that there was an unlimited demand for the produce which he could raise, that, in fact, the enterprise had in it all the elements of success; suppose all this, but suppose also that he was the only planter in that portion of the globe who had ever embarked in such an enterprise, and what would be the exchange value of his estate? It is quite evident that if he wanted to sell it he would find no purchaser. Possibly, after he had demonstrated that his enterprise was a successful one, when, in fact, it had ceased to be an enterprise at all, he would find purchasers enough. But can it be said that, till then, his property had no industrial value? The inventor's labour-saving machine, the emigrant's plough, and the planter's estate, had all of them value in this sense, independent altogether of their exchangeability. Their industrial value was antecedent to their value in exchange, and the latter was the effect, not the cause, of the former. Value in use is the basis of industrial activity; without it there would be no production, and without production there could be no exchange. To limit value by exchange, then, is to deprive Economic Science of the very foundation on which the whole superstructure rests.

Utility, and difficulty of attainment.

According to Mill, there are two elements essential to value, namely, utility, and difficulty of attainment, or scarcity.[1] But these two elements do not of themselves constitute value. An article may be useful, and at the same time valueless. Water, for instance, is an element necessary to human existence, and is therefore in the highest degree useful. But it does not on that account possess value. An article may also be exceedingly scarce and yet be perfectly valueless, as, for instance, certain kinds of metals

[1] Senior and Prof. Cairnes maintain there are three, namely, utility, difficulty of attainment, and transferableness. But surely transferableness is included in the term exchange value.

and minerals well-known to chemists, which I need not here enumerate. And even difficulty of attainment combined with utility will not confer value on an article. Water, though useful, and ever so scarce, as in the case of a traveller in an arid desert, does not have any value conferred on it on that account, if the traveller does not want it. But if he wanted it, if he was thirsty, and if he believed that it would satisfy his thirst, water would then be immediately invested with a value in his estimation which neither its acknowledged utility nor its inaccessibility or scarcity previously conferred. A threshing machine is an article which possesses utility, though of a different kind; but in the eyes of a native of Tierra del Fuego, even if he had its uses explained to him, and was assured that it was the only article of its kind in his country, it would have no value if he did not want to use it. Pure air is necessary to health, and is therefore useful; but though I may know that it is so, and may be perfectly assured that the air I constantly breathe is not pure, and that pure air is perfectly unattainable in the unwholesome atmosphere in which I live, still I may attach no value to it. But if I knew its use and at the same time wanted it, I would probably give up my business or profession and go abroad in order to obtain it; in other words, I might value it so much as to sacrifice my prospects for life in order to possess it.

Human desire, then, I maintain, is the essence of value. We value an object because we believe its possession will satisfy a desire, and we desire to possess or retain possession of an object only when we believe possession will be useful or agreeable to us, that is to say, confer pleasure or remove pain. The deprivation of the means of enjoyment creates pain, the possession of these means creates pleasure. Thus, whatever creates pleasure or removes pain becomes an object of desire and therefore of value. First, in the order of time, comes the pain of deprivation, or the pleasure of possession; next, the mind, connecting the feeling of pain or pleasure with an object capable, or supposed to be capable, of removing the one or conferring the other, desires to obtain or retain possession of that object. Thus the deprivation of food creates pain; the mind, connecting the pain with an object, food, believed to be capable of relieving the pain, desires its possession. The deprivation of wealth creates all the pains incident to poverty, as physical privation, toil, impotence, and indignity; and we desire the removal of these by the possession of the means which wealth places at our command. It is hardly correct, however, to speak of utility or difficulty of attainment as elements at all, for they are simply factors in the calculation by which the mind forms its estimate of the desirableness of an object.

Essential character of value.

As compared with utility, difficulty of attainment is a subordinate or accidental factor in value, as the latter only helps to direct the mind to the former. When deprived of a thing

Difficulty of attainment subordinate to utility.

which is useful to us we are then forcibly impressed with its utility, which, but for the deprivation, might otherwise have been overlooked. Utility, on the other hand, is an essential factor, as the value of a thing depends on its utility. Nevertheless, utility is not value. We value a thing because it is desirable; and the more desirable a thing is the more valuable it is, and the less desirable the less valuable. But it is desirable because we believe it to be useful, that is to say, capable of satisfying a desire. Utility may exist apart from desire, but desire cannot exist apart from utility.

Definition of value.

We cannot, therefore, speak of inherent or intrinsic value. Value does not exist in the object desired, but in the mind. It is not an objective but a subjective quality. It is not a quality "in a thing," as Senior defines it, but a purely mental attribute. If value were a quality existing in a thing, all objects would have everywhere and at all times the same value. But the same object may be both valuable and valueless to different individuals, and even to the same individuals at different times and at different places. An object may be valuable to one man and not to another; it may even be valuable and worthless to the same man at different times and under different circumstances. To a hungry man food is valuable; to the same man dying of thirst it has no value whatever. Again, if by value we mean exchange value, we should be able to exchange equally everywhere: so many yards or pounds of one commodity would exchange for so many yards or pounds of another. Value, or rather price, would then not be determined by demand and supply, as all articles would have their true value stamped upon them, and would exchange themselves, as it were, automatically. Value is that quality or attribute with which the mind invests an object capable, or supposed to be capable, of satisfying a desire. It is, in fact, desirableness.

So far we have treated of value in use, which I conceive to be true value. Value in exchange, or exchange value, on the other hand, is not value at all, but Price. The exchange value of a thing is what that thing will fetch in the market, that is, its price, which is something altogether from its value. Value is an absolute, not a relative term; price, on the other hand, is a relative and not an absolute term. The value of a thing is what that thing is worth to me; the price of a thing, on the other hand, is what some one else will give me for it. Exchange value we shall therefore consider in the following chapter when we treat of price.

CHAPTER VIII.

ON PRICE.

When we come to exchange, or to actual transactions in the market, it is no longer with value but with price that we have to deal. The essential difference between value and price consists in this, that while the former is a single estimate, the latter is a double estimate, the estimate of a buyer or buyers on the one side, and of a seller or sellers on the other. The price of a thing is what it will fetch in the market;[1] and while there is only one price at a given time and place, there are always several values. A price can only be arrived at when two or more values coincide, or

Difference between value and price.

[1] Here we have another illustration of the scientific misappropriation of terms in common use. *Value*, according to Mill (and his followers have one and all endorsed his definition), means "exchange value," that is to say *Price* (*Principles*, book iii. ch. v. 1), whereas *Price* he defines as "value in money," or monetary consideration (book iii. ch. i. 2). Now *Value* (from *valere*, to be sound, to be worth or worthy) properly means worth, estimate, or utility; and *Price* (from *prendre*, to take or seize) has the same meaning that he gives to *Value*, namely, exchange value, "that which is taken in purchase or payment." (Richardson.)

when the estimate put upon an article by a seller agrees with the estimate put upon it by a buyer. Not only do individuals differ in their values, but they have different methods of arriving at them. One man may estimate an article according to the use he can make of it, that is, its true value; another man may estimate an article according to its scarcity, that is, monopoly value; a third may estimate it according to its cost of production, which is variously called its necessary, natural, or nominal value. The market, however, is the true test of all these values.

How price is determined.

The market price is arrived at by a comparison of individual values. I value a commodity which I desire to sell, and I also value the commodity which I desire to get in exchange for it. The person who desires to buy my commodity or sell another commodity to me likewise puts his value on both. If my value is the same as his, the equation of our values will be the price. But if our values do not agree, if he demands more than I am willing to give, or I demand more than he is willing to give me in exchange for what I have, and if neither of us will give way, there will be no exchange, and therefore no price.

Price may also be said to be determined by Correlative Demand. Each party to an exchange demands so much of one commodity for so much of another. If the demands are equal, the equation of the two demands will be the price or rate at which the exchange will be effected; if unequal, no price can be quoted, unless the demands of the one rise or fall to the demands of the other, when a price will be fixed at that point.

Economists usually speak of demand as something quite different from supply. Demand they regard as a qualificative, supply as a quantitative element; the former as having reference to desire, the latter to quantity supplied. To speak of the ratio between demand and supply, in the sense in which these terms are understood, is absurd, for, as Mill asks, What ratio can there be between two things not of the same denomination, as a quantity and desire? "A ratio between a demand and a supply," he says, "is only intelligible if by demand we mean the quantity demanded, and if the ratio intended is between the quantity demanded and the quantity supplied."[1] This is undoubtedly true; there cannot be a desire on the one side and a supply or quantity on the other, and it is perfectly evident there cannot be quantity on both sides apart from desire.

Demand and supply in relation to price.

To get rid of this difficulty, Mill accordingly reduces both elements to the same denomination, and explains *Demand* to mean "the quantity demanded," and *Supply*, "the quantity offered for sale."[2] As the expression "offered for sale" implies demand on the side of the seller, both

Mill's definition of the terms *Demand* and *Supply*.

[1] *Principles*, vol. i. book iii. ch. ii. 4.

[2] To the same effect Prof. Jenkins defines supply as "quantity holders are willing to sell," and demand as "quantity buyers are willing to purchase." See *Essay on Demand and Supply* in *Recess Studies*, pp. 151-2.

elements may now be said to be denominationally the same, but, instead of there being one element on each side, there are now two: a desire and a quantity, and a quantity and a desire. But this does not help to elucidate matters much. Is the ratio to be between the desire on the one side and the quantity on the other; or does quantity go against quantity, and desire against desire? Mill saw that he was involving himself in a difficulty here, for he goes on to say, "But the quantity demanded is not a fixed quantity, even at the same time and place; it varies according to the value: if the thing is cheap, there is usually a demand for more of it than when it is dear. The demand, therefore, partly depends on the value. But it was before laid down that the value depends on the demand. From this contradiction how shall we extricate ourselves? How solve the paradox of two things each depending upon the other?"[1] There is no solution possible. If the quantity "varies according to the value," clearly the value cannot be determined by the quantity. It is a contradiction in terms. But there is really no necessity for rendering the subject more complex by introducing the element of quantity at all, for the mental process indicated by the term Demand is quite sufficient to explain all the phenomena. It is demand on both sides. The buyer demands, and the seller demands likewise; and the demand is the same in both cases, for the object con-

[1] *Principles*, vol. i. book iii. ch. ii. 3.

templated is an exchange of commodities. If quantity be imported into the question at all, it must only be as a subordinate or accidental element, for in no sense can it rank with desire, or even with utility. At the most, it is only a cause of a cause; it may influence utility in the same manner as utility influences demand. If a man has a larger quantity of any commodity than he requires, this fact may predispose him to get rid of a portion of it, or make him desirous to sell. In other words, quantity may influence demand in proportion as it affects the utility of the commodity.

Demand and *Supply* not suitable terms.

The fact of the matter is, the terms *Demand* and *Supply* do not properly express the nature of the process which takes place when commodities are exchanged in the open market. The word *Demand*, as we have said, signifies desire, but the term *Supply* signifies a stock, provision, or quantity provided. The word *Supply* is therefore not the correlative of *Demand;* the latter indicates a mental process, while the former has no such meaning. If *Supply* is the correct word, then its correlative is not *Demand*, but some word indicating absence of supply.[1] On the other hand, if *Demand* is the correct word, its correlate is not *Supply*, but some other term, expressive of the mental process which takes place when anything is "offered for sale." What is that mental process? It

[1] The correlative of *Supply*, in Parliamentary phraseology, is *Expenditure*—income as distinguished from outcome, if I may be permitted the expression.

is the same, exactly, that takes place on the other side. The seller desires or demands, just the same as the buyer. The buyer desires to buy, and the seller desires to sell, and it is demand on both sides. There is no difference in the mental process between the one and the other, and the object aimed at by both is exactly the same, namely, exchange of commodities. If a seller desired to sell, and no one desired to buy, or if the buyer desired to buy, and no one desired to sell, no exchange would take place. In other words, both are demanders, as each desires something which the other has; and, in the same sense, both are suppliers, as each comes provided with something to offer in exchange for that which he desires to obtain.

Correlative demand.

There is really no necessity for importing into the question the element of quantity at all. The whole of the confusion has arisen from the use of the word *Supply*. If instead of the words *Demand* and *Supply* we used the term *Correlative Demand,* all would be clear. And this, as I have said, is the only correct way of expressing the mental process involved in exchange. Supply, in the sense of offered for sale, or placed on the market, is really a demand for something in exchange for that offered, precisely in the same way, and to the same extent, as Demand is an offer to supply something in exchange for that demanded. The seller has one kind of commodity and the buyer has another, and they mutually demand an exchange.

Suppose, however, that Mill's definition were the

correct one, and that supply, in the sense of quantity offered for sale, regulated prices; it would then follow that the price of a commodity would vary in exact proportion to the increase or decrease of the quantity of that commodity placed on the market. If the supply fell one-third, the price would rise in the same proportion, that is, exactly one-third; on the other hand, if the supply increased one-third, the price would fall one-third, and so on, the price falling and rising in exact proportion to the quantity supplied. I need scarcely say that, as a matter of fact, prices do not rise and fall in this fashion. Take the oft-quoted case of corn, for instance. As pointed out by Tooke, the price of this commodity has risen in England from 100 to 200 per cent. and upwards, when the utmost computed deficiency in the crops has not been more than between one-sixth and one-third below average, and when that deficiency had been relieved by foreign supplies.[1] After a full review of the whole phenomena of price, as affected by quantity supplied, the only approach to a "law" which the author of the *History of Prices* was able to arrive at was the very general one that "if there should be a deficiency of the crops amounting to one-third, without any surplus from a former year, and without any chance of relief from importation, the price might rise five, six, and even seven fold."

Quantitativeness not an essential element in price.

The case of a deficiency.

[1] *History of Prices*, vol. i. p. 13.

The case of a surplus.

Reverse the case, and assume that there is a surplus instead of a deficiency. Let us suppose that the ordinary consumption of a country is, say, one million of bushels, the average price 5*s.* per bushel, and that the crop of wheat in a given year yielded just double that quantity, namely, two millions of bushels. The farmers could then afford to sell the two millions of bushels at about one-half the price they could the one million, making due allowance, of course, for extra expenses in harvesting, storing, and bringing to market the larger quantity. If the farmers were all well off they would, if they could not find a market abroad, hold over their surplus till the following year; that is to say, there would be no urgent desire to sell, and prices would not only not fall one-half, but they would not fall at all, or very little. On the other hand, if the farmers were not well off, if they were in debt, if their necessities were pressing, they would desire to sell as quickly as possible. There would then be more sellers than buyers in the market; the demand to sell would be greater than the demand to buy, and prices would fall. But the cause of the fall would not be the excess of the supply for that would have been held over till another year, but the necessities of the farmers, or the greater demand to sell as compared with the lesser demand to buy.

Any excess or deficiency in the quantity of any commodity at any given time or place only affects prices by predisposing holders to sell or to buy. The absence of sufficient storage accommodation may, for example, induce a farmer to take a much lower price for his crop than he otherwise would. In England, during the thirteenth and fourteenth centuries, and even much later, the farmers were without capital, the trade of the corn-dealer was then unknown, and the only storage accommodation for grain in any considerable quantity was in the Abbey Granges.[1] The consequence of this state of things was that the farmer had to dispose of his crop at low prices immediately after harvest. The price of corn in those days was almost always extremely low at harvest time, and invariably rose as the year advanced, and frequently to an enormous height just before next harvest. It is related by Stow, that in 1317 wheat, which before harvest was selling at £4 per quarter, fell immediately the crop was got in to 6*s.* 8*d.* per quarter, or to one-twelfth its previous price. Here it might be said that the absence of accommodation was the cause of the reduction, and the statement would be quite as correct as to say that it was the excess of supply; but the absence of accommodation only affected the price by increasing the demand for a market, and this increased demand was the true cause of the fall in price.

Effects of an excess or deficiency of commodities.

Precisely the same effect takes place in the money market when there is a pressing necessity for money;

[1] Eden, *State of the Poor*, vol. i. p. 18.

Fluctuations in the money market.

that is to say, the price rises, but here again not in proportion to the deficiency of supply, or indeed on account of the supply at all, but in proportion, and in exact proportion, to the demand. Mr. Bagehot thus explains the cause of a rise in the price of money. "Up to a certain point," he says, "money is a necessity. If a merchant has acceptances to meet to-morrow, money he must and will find to-day, at some price or other. And it is the urgent need of the whole body of merchants which runs up the value of money so wildly and to such a height in a great panic."[1] Here, there was no deficiency, or anticipated deficiency, in the supply; there was no sudden withdrawal of gold from the country. The money was in the banks, or in the hands of the bill-discounters, in quantity, it must be presumed, sufficient for ordinary business requirements. But there was a sudden increase in the demand for it to meet the urgent requirements of the merchants. True, it may be said, but the sudden increase in the demand was due to a previous scarcity, a large amount of money having been already invested, or wasted in wild speculation, and was therefore not immediately available. But if a larger quantity of money than usual had been previously invested, this, again, could only have been caused by an antecedent demand for it, so that whichever way we look at the matter we still come back to demand as the cause.

---

[1] *Lombard Street*, p. 119.

Has quantity, or difficulty of attainment, then, no effect upon price? The answer is that it may or it may not. In the first place, it is not the actual quantity in existence, or the actual quantity in the market, that we have to deal with, but what we *think* is the quantity; and, in the second place, it is not only what we think the quantity is, but this combined with what we think it *ought* to be. The stock of any commodity may be much less than we believe it to be, and if so there will be no corresponding increase in price; or it may be much larger than we believe it to be, and if so there will be no corresponding reduction. It is opinion that influences prices, and that opinion may be founded on a correct knowledge of the state of the market, or it may not; but in either case the result is the same. If a seller thinks there is a deficiency of any commodity, he may increase his price for that commodity; if he thinks there is a surplus, he may reduce his price. If a purchaser believes there is a surplus of any commodity, he will demand a reduction in price, for he knows that some holder will submit to a sacrifice rather than have his stock left on his hands; if he believes there is a deficiency, he will be eager to buy, and to buy at an advanced price, as he thinks he will still be able to resell at a profit.

Quantity in relation to price.

But in saying this much on behalf of quantitativeness I am giving it far more prominence than it is really entitled to, for it does not follow that a commodity will be high or low in price because it is scarce or plentiful.

There may be a great increase in the quantity and no corresponding decrease in the price; and there may be a great decrease in the quantity and no corresponding increase in the price. A decrease in price is even compatible with a decrease in quantity, and an increase in price with an increase in quantity. Practically, buying and selling is seldom regulated by quantity at all. A buyer finds sellers eager to sell, and he does not, as a rule, inquire into the cause of this eagerness. It is enough for him that it exists, that he can purchase readily what he wants; and he naturally concludes that when there are many eager to sell he will get what he wants at a reduced price, and he acts accordingly. A seller finds buyers eager to buy, and he does not inquire into the cause of this eagerness, but accepts the fact, and consequently increases his price. It is demand, therefore, and not quantity, that determines price. And if we go behind demand and inquire what influences demand, we shall find that quantitativeness is only one cause out of many, as demand may be influenced by a variety of causes. Demand, for instance, may be influenced by the financial position of the seller. The phrases "held well" and "held weakly," so familiar on the stock exchange, illustrate what I mean. Stock is said to be "held well" when it is in good hands, or in the possession of those who can hold it till they can get their own price, and in such a case, no matter how large an amount of stock so held or offered for sale, the price will be maintained. "Held weakly," on the other hand, is stock that is in bad hands, or in the possession of those who will be forced to sell sooner or later, and in such a case the price is likely to decline. Demand may also be influenced by fashion; and again the demand for one commodity may be influenced by the demand for another commodity, as for example, when there is a great demand for the necessaries of life there is very little demand for labour.[1] But, indeed, it is quite unnecessary to follow up this part of the inquiry, for the causes which influence demand are almost infinite in number and variety. It would be just as reasonable to inquire into the causes which influence desire, which are as numerous as there are objects and ends which are desirable.

[1] See p. 48.

CHAPTER IX.

ON PRICE (CONTINUED).

Instruments of production.

So far I have treated only of the prices of commodities which are exchanged the one for the other, but now I come to consider a class of commodities, or instruments of production, which are not themselves exchanged, but only the right to use them. These are Labour, Capital, and Land. When a man gives his services in exchange for wages, for instance, he does not part outright with anything, he only sells, or exchanges, the use of what he still possesses, namely, his physical and mental faculties. These are still his own, and those who have the temporary use of them are held responsible for their safe keeping. It is the same with Capital and Land, which are not exchanged, but only hired, and the hirer has to return them again to their owner unimpaired in quantity or quality.

Labour.

The wages of labour, Mill tells us, depend mainly on "demand and supply," or on "the proportion between population and capital."[1] Here, again, the

[1] *Principles*, vol. i. book ii. ch. x. 1.

element of quantity crops up in a new and unexpected shape, for now we have not only a quantity on one, but on both sides; that is to say, if we are to understand by the term Population mere numbers, and by the term Capital simply quantity or amount of money available. Indeed, Mill leaves us in no doubt as to his meaning, for he goes on to explain that "by population is here meant the number only of the labouring class, or, rather, of those who work for hire; and by capital, only circulating capital, and not even the whole of that, but the part which is expended in the direct purchase of labour." How, may I venture to ask, can "demand and supply" regulate wages, if wages are determined by the "proportion between population and capital" in the sense explained as above? How, again, can there be any "demand" between a number and a quantity; and how can there be any ratio between a quantity and a demand, or, for that matter, between a quantity and a number?

The wages-fund theory.

But not only is quantity introduced as an element on both sides, but special pains have been taken to limit the meaning of the term Capital. By capital is meant only that portion of the circulating capital "expended in the direct purchase of labour," or, in other words, the wages fund. This theory of a wages fund has experienced many vicissitudes in recent times, but it manages still to maintain its footing in certain quarters. The theory originated with Mill, or, at all events, he was the first who elaborated it, and for about a quarter of a century it was an unquestioned article of faith among his followers.[1] The theory was first called in question by Mr. Longe; it was subsequently condemned by Mr. Thornton, and ultimately repudiated by its author, who professed himself convinced by Mr. Thornton's arguments against it. Now, however, Prof. Cairnes steps on the scene, and, after reviewing the whole controversy, expresses his surprise that Mill should have been so easily convinced, and announces that, in his opinion, the theory is perfectly unassailable. But with all due deference to such a high authority as Prof. Cairnes, I venture to say that if the principles of Political Economy were no more unassailable than this wages-fund theory, they would stand but a poor chance of surviving.

Based on erroneous assumptions.

The advocates of the wages-fund theory assume, first, that the capital of a country is a fixed quantity, and that the capital employed in industry is a fixed proportion of this quantity; and, secondly, that wages are paid out of that portion of capital which is set apart for industry. Both of these propositions, in my opinion, are erroneous.

That the capital of a country is a fixed quantity.

With regard to the first, namely, that the capital of a country is a fixed quantity, and that the amount employed in industry is a fixed proportion of this quantity, I have only to

[1] Adam Smith, indeed, speaks of "a fund destined for the payment of wages," but he enters into no explanation. See *Wealth of Nations*, book i. ch. viii. and elsewhere.

say that there is no fact in Economic Science so well established as this, that capital follows profits. If the profits of a country are large, capital will flow into it; if small, capital will withdraw from it, and seek investment elsewhere where profits are larger. Capital is always forthcoming wherever there are prospects of large profits. In order to procure capital for such investments, personal expenses are cut down, money lying idle is collected, property is realized, and credit strained to the utmost. The capital of a country, therefore, is not a fixed quantity, for if its credit is good, and sufficient inducements are offered in the shape of interest, it can readily borrow whatever it wants. For the same reason the capital employed in industry is not a fixed quantity, and varies, not in proportion to the gross amount in the country, but in proportion to the profitableness of the industry of that country.

That wages are paid out of capital.

With regard to the second proposition, namely, that wages are paid out of capital, this is true to a limited extent only. No doubt a certain amount of capital is required for the payment of wages, just as a certain amount of capital is necessary for the purchase of raw material, though we never heard of a special fund for the purchase of the latter. There is this essential difference between the two cases, however, that while raw material is paid for (in cash or in bills) before being used, wages are not paid till they have been earned. The employer has the benefit of the labourer's services before, and sometimes long before, he is called upon to pay for them. The day labourer is not paid his wages till the conclusion of his day's work. The workman who is hired by the week gives his employer the benefit of his services from one to six days before the latter is called upon to pay for them. The merchant or retail trader who pays for his labour by the month; the farmer who pays half-yearly or yearly; and the shipowner who pays at the end of the voyage, which may be for twelve or eighteen months, have had, day by day, week by week, and month by month, the full benefit of their employés' services, with profits added, before being called on to pay a fraction of wages. The employé, in fact, stands to his employer in the relation of a capitalist who advances him the use of his services, and which services are ultimately paid for, not out of a wages fund, but out of the produce of the services themselves.

Relation of profits to wages.

In order to understand the relation between capital and labour, we have only to ask what is the object of an employer when he hires labour. The employer does not hire labour because he has a fund set apart for the payment of wages which he otherwise would not know what to do with, but because he sees his way to making a profit out of it—profit being the difference between two prices, the price, namely, at which a thing is bought, on the one hand, and the price at which it is sold, on the other. As long as there is a margin of profit between the wages paid for labour and the produce of that labour, so long will labour be employed, and no longer. Of course, I am speaking of productive labour only, for the demand for non-productive labour is not influenced by profits, but by income or capital, a distinction which the advocates of the wages-fund theory have apparently not observed. Hence, instead of saying with Ricardo and Fawcett[1] that a rise in profits can never be brought about except by a fall in the rate of wages, or a fall in profits except by a corresponding rise in the rate of wages, I should rather say that, wherever labour is free and the wages-earning classes intelligent, a rise in the rate of wages will generally be the result of a rise in profits, and a fall in the rate of wages the result of a fall in profits.

Case of the iron and coal trades.

I am only surprised that any one who is conversant with the industrial history of the day can entertain a different opinion. That high wages are the result of high profits, and *vice versâ*, every one at all acquainted with modern wages disputes will acknowledge at once. The history of the coal and iron trades disputes in England for the last dozen years shows that whenever the price of either of these commodities was low, the rate of the wages of those employed in their production was low also, and whenever the price was high the rate of wages was high in proportion. Take, for instance, the price of iron and the

[1] Prof. Fawcett, indeed, goes so far as to assert that "it is physically impossible that a permanent rise of wages should take place without a corresponding diminution of profits."—*Manual of Political Economy*, p. 264. To talk of *physical* impossibility in connection with the laws of wages is surely science run mad.

wages of iron workers and colliers during the last few years. From midsummer, 1871, Scotch pig-iron advanced steadily from 57*s.* 6*d.* per ton, till February, 1873, when it reached 145*s.* per ton. Of course, the profits of the ironmasters when the latter figure ruled were enormous. The high profits induced the ironmasters to make extraordinary efforts to keep their furnaces going to the utmost extent of their capacity. But to do this required an increased supply of labour, to meet which there was an increase in the demand, and a corresponding increase in the rate of wages. Thus we find that the wages of puddlers, ironworkers, and colliers (coal being largely used in the manufacture of iron, the price of the latter commodity influences the wages of colliers as well) advanced steadily with the price of iron, rising, in February, 1873, from 50 to 60 per cent. above what they were in midsummer, 1871. But towards the end of 1874 the price of iron receded. In December of that year it fell to 76*s.* 6*d.* per ton, and wages were immediately affected by the reduction, colliers' wages falling 25 to 30 per cent., puddlers' and ironworkers' 27½ per cent., below what they were in February, 1873.[1]

[1] "As wages have such an important connection with the price of iron, it is worth noting the changes which have taken place during the last three years. Starting with midsummer, 1871, it may be assumed that the advance in colliers' wages generally was not less than 50 to 60 per cent. (In Scotland the advance was greater, but late reductions have been in like proportion.) The reductions throughout the various districts, though neither uniform as regards time nor amount, may be estimated at about 20 to 25 per cent., so that wages now are probably about 25 per cent. to 30 per cent. higher than the lowest rate paid prior

A few extracts, culled at random from the trade correspondence in the metropolitan journals, will show

to 1871. The puddlers and ironworkers have submitted to two reductions of 10 per cent., which (less 2½ per cent. advance in July quarter) is equal to 17½ per cent. reduction during the year, and as a further reduction of 10 per cent. is announced, this will be a reduction in all of 27½ per cent. A reduction of 1*s*. per ton in puddling will bring the rate down to 9*s*. 9*d*. per ton, whilst by the 'Derby' agreement the minimum was fixed at 9*s*. 6*d*. per ton. The arrangement is terminable on 1st July, 1875, if desired. Having made a comparison of wages during the past three years, it may be instructive to place alongside of this the fluctuations in iron. Scotch G.M.B. warrants, which were 57*s*. 6*d*. in midsummer, 1871, advanced to 145*s*. in February, 1873, from which they have receded to 76*s*. 6*d*. on 31st December, 1874. Welsh bar iron, which was £7 f.o.b. Liverpool at midsummer, 1871, advanced to £13, from which it has receded to £8 15*s*. at close of 1874."—*Commercial History* of 1874, in the *Economist.*

Another illustration to the same effect comes from the other side of the Atlantic:—"We have not yet done paying the penalty for false prosperity which followed the war and will continue through the paper-money period. All kinds of business are very much prostrated. The capitalists are accepting lower rates of interest, and the holders of stock investments are generally becoming satisfied with 6 per cent. interest and even 5 per cent., if the payment of that smaller rate is fully assured. Hundreds and thousands are out of employment, and all, rich and poor, are gradually coming down to humbler pretensions. As a marked evidence of this fact we notice that President Gowen, of the Reading Railroad and the Reading Coal and Iron Company, on the 28th inst. issued a circular to all clerks, agents, and employés of the companies named, notifying them that on the 1st of September, 1876, a general reduction in wages in all departments will be made as follows:—Upon all persons receiving less than 2000 dols. per annum, a reduction of 10 per cent. Upon those receiving from 2000 dols. to 5000 dols. per annum, a reduction of 15 per cent. Upon those receiving from 5000 to 10,000 dols. per annum, a reduction of 20 per cent. Upon all receiving over 10,000 dols. per annum, a reduction of 30 per cent. This reduction of salaries applies to the salaries of President Gowen and the Vice-Presidents, as well as to the most humble trackman or switch-tender, and is based on the principle that the higher the salary the greater the percentage of reduction."—*Philadelphia Ledger*, August 31st, 1876.

that the close relation that exists between prices and wages is well understood by practical men. Thus a Darlington correspondent writes:—"The declining rates of iron within 1874 are indicated not merely by the relative prices now and at the beginning of January, 1873, but also by the *reduction of the wages* of malleable ironworkers within that period by 35 per cent., the last reduction of 10 per cent. being declared on Friday."[1] A Sheffield correspondent says:—"*The prices of iron have latterly fallen to such an extent that it is feared the revised list for labour will not meet the requirements of the case.* Blast-furnace men will, in a day or two, receive 5 per cent. less wages and ironworkers 6 per cent. Even with these concessions in their favour, masters will be unable to manufacture common material excepting with a very low margin of profit. Many of the ironmasters here are proprietors of coal-pits, and, in order to push the iron trade, they are willing at last to reduce rates for fuel. But the case is urgent, and they have given notice to the miners of an immediate revision of the wages list. The men are expected to make a concession of 10 per cent., but they are very unwilling to do so."[2] And, again—"There is great uneasiness as to the future of the coal trade. The masters of South Yorkshire and North Derbyshire, as already stated in *Iron*, determined to reduce the colliers' wages by 10 per cent. *The men have declined to make the concession, on the ground that*

[1] *The Times*, January 4th, 1875.
[2] *Iron*, August 4th, 1875.

'*trade is more active than it was*,' and suggest the continuance of the present tariff of remuneration. The employers are now considering the matter, and the aspect of affairs is very serious, as they are combined, rich, and, with the market in a dull condition, in a position to enforce their notice."[1] A Barrow-in-Furness correspondent writes:— "The fact that at one or two of the large manufacturing establishments in this district makers have given notice of a further reduction in the earnings of their workmen *displays the position into which manufacturers have been driven by the gradual reduction which has been made in the value of iron.* Prices have been reduced to the lowest point, and it seems imminent that if any further reduction is effected a crisis will ensue, unless makers are content to work without profit."[2]

So well known, in fact, is the effect of profits on wages, that the price of coal and iron has, of late years, come to be acknowledged as the standard by which the wages of those employed in the production and manufacture of those commodities should be regulated, and a tariff of wages based on the price of iron has now been in existence in the iron trade for some years.

Variations in the rate of wages in different countries.

Prof. Cairnes seems to think the wages-fund theory is also necessary in order to explain the variations in the rate of wages in different countries, for he asks, How otherwise can we account for the fact that there is one rate for

[1] *Iron*, September 4th, 1875.
[2] *Ibid.* August 21st, 1875.

the United States, another rate for Great Britain, and another for the continent of Europe?[1] But the difficulty rather is to discover what connection the wages-fund theory can have with the matter at issue. On the principle here stated the question resolves itself solely into one of profit. In every question of wages there are two parties concerned, the party demanding employment, and the party demanding labour. If the profits of any business are large, and these profits can be maintained and increased by the employment of more labour, labour will be in demand and wages will consequently rise; if, on the other hand, profits are small, there will be little demand for labour, and wages will fall. Adam Smith perceived the point clearly enough when he said: "It is not the actual greatness of natural wealth, but its continual increase, which occasions a rise in the wages of labour. It is not, accordingly, in the richest countries, but in the most thriving, or in those which are growing rich the fastest, that the wages of labour are the highest."[2]

Special causes of variation.

If the labourers of any country are entirely dependent on wages for their subsistence, wages will generally be low, but if they have other means of subsistence, if they can employ their own labour with advantage to themselves, wages will generally be high. Wages are higher in the United States than in

[1] *Some Leading Questions*, part ii. ch. i.
[2] *Wealth of Nations*, book i. ch. viii.

Great Britain, and higher in Great Britain than on the continent of Europe; and it is to be noted that in those countries where they are high, profits are high also, while at the same time the condition of the labourer is far more independent than in those countries where wages are low. In the United States the labourers who are dissatisfied with the rate of wages offered them have the alternative of going West and taking up land;[1] and in the State of California and in Australia, where wages are much higher than in the Eastern and Middle States, they have, in addition to the facilities afforded them by liberal land laws, the opportunity of going to the gold fields. The prevalence of the allotment system in England during the middle ages will explain how it was that the agricultural labouring population in this country were better provided, as Hallam informs us they were, with the means of subsistence than they are now.[2] From the Anglo-Saxon period to the reign of Henry VII. nearly the entire population of England derived their subsistence immediately from the soil, and every labourer had a small croft or parcel of land attached to his dwelling, with the right of turning out a cow or a few

---

[1] "'Sir,' said to me a Minnesota farmer, 'the curse of this country is that we have too much land;' a phrase which I have heard again and again—among the iron-masters of Pittsburg, among the tobacco-planters of Richmond, among the cotton-spinners of Worcester. Indeed, this wail against the land is common among men who, having mines, plantations, mills, and farms, would like to have large supplies of labour at lower rates of wages than the market yields."—*New America*, p. 221, 8th edition.

[2] *History of the Middle Ages*, iii. 372, edition 1855; also, Eden's *State of the Poor*, vol. i. p. 32.

pigs or sheep into the woods, commons, or wastes of the manor. All this was changed, however, by the consolidation of small farms in the sixteenth century, and subsequently by the enclosure of commons and waste lands, which completed the process by which the labourer was thrown for his sole dependence on money wages.[1] In Great Britain and on the continent of Europe, on the other hand, there are, at the present day, no such facilities; there are no gold mines, land is excessively dear, and the labourer is consequently compelled to accept the wages his employer is pleased to give.[2]

---

[1] "The extent to which the subdivision of the soil was at one time carried in England may be understood from the following illustration:—The occupation of the land on a farm called Holt, in the parish of Clapham, Sussex, consisting of 160 acres, has been traced since the thirteenth century up to the present time. During the thirteenth and fourteenth centuries this farm, which is now occupied by one tenant, was a hamlet, and there is a document in existence which contains twenty-one distinct conveyances of land in fee, described as parcels of this land. In 1400 the number of proprietors began to decrease; by the year 1520 it had been reduced to six; in the reign of James I. the six were reduced to two; and soon after the Restoration the whole became the property of one owner, who let it as a farm to one tenant."—*Quarterly Review*, No. 81, p. 250.

[2] "People who have at home some kind of property to apply their labour to, will not sell their labour for wages that do not afford them a better diet than potatoes and maize, although, in saving for themselves, they may live very much on potatoes and maize. We are often surprised, in travelling on the continent, to hear of a rate of day's wages very high, considering the abundance and cheapness of food. It is the want of necessity or inclination to take work that makes a day's labour scarce, and consequently the price of provisions is dear, in many parts of the continent, where property in land is widely diffused among the people."—Laing's *Notes of a Traveller*, p. 456.

The same principle which influences the rate of wages in various countries determines also the variations in the same country and in the same trade or profession. Why do we pay high wages to a good workman and low wages to a bad one? Why do we give a large fee to one member of a profession and a small one to another member of the same profession? Obviously because it is profitable to do so. It is more profitable to give a labourer seven shillings a day who can remove thirty cubic yards of earth, than five shillings per day to another who can only remove half that quantity. It is more profitable to give a bricklayer ten shillings a day who can lay two thousand bricks, than eight shillings a day to one who can only lay one thousand. It is more profitable, taking into account the risk at stake, for a suitor, in a case involving important issues, to employ a barrister of proved ability at one hundred guineas, than to give ten guineas to a junior member of the same profession to conduct the case. There may be any number of briefless barristers ready to undertake the case at the lesser fee, but no suitor in his senses would entrust it to them. It is the amount of profit that is to be made, or, what is the same thing, the amount of loss that is to be avoided, that influences the demand for such services.

Variations in the same country.

But, apart from the wages-fund theory, the inoperativeness of demand and supply, in a quantitative sense, upon market price, may be illustrated by the case of a reserve. If a

Wages are regulated by profits.

quantity of employment is offered upon which a certain rate is placed, and a quantity of labour is required, whether more or less than the quantity offered is immaterial, at a certain rate, and if the two rates agree, the result will be a contract, and the terms of this contract will be the price of wages. But if the reserve placed upon their labour by the workmen is higher than the employers are able to give, as employers will not carry on business at a loss, no contract will be entered into, although the workmen desire employment and the employers desire labour. The quantities were present on both sides, but no price was fixed, because neither side would agree to the terms offered. What would follow would be a dead-lock, a strike or a lock-out, as the case might be; but, as there were no means of compelling either employers or workmen to accept the terms offered, the dispute could only terminate when the demand on the one side exceeded in intensity (not in quantity) the demand on the other. As in mechanics the strength of a work lies in its weakest part, so in this case the weakest part on either side would be that which would give way, and the part that would give way would be that on which the pressure was greatest compared with the power of resistance. In other words, if the necessities of a single workman or a single employer compelled him to accept the terms offered, the whole dispute would be at an end. So well is this understood by both employers and workmen, that the former always trust to the chance of one or more workmen being driven by necessity to accept their terms; and the workmen, when they attempt a strike, always try it on with a weak employer before making it general in the trade.

Capital is also an instrument which is not transferred or exchanged but only used. The man who borrows capital pays for the right to use it in the shape of interest, and in the shape of rent if the capital had been previously invested in some kind of property.

Capital.

The price of money, or the rate of interest, does not depend on its quantity, as even Mill acknowledges,[1] although somewhat inconsistently, as I consider; for why should not the price of money be regulated in the same manner as the price of any other commodity? Money is subject to the same fluctuations as ordinary commodities, and its price ought to be regulated in the same way, namely, by demand; and demand, again, is influenced, as in the case of ordinary commodities, by profits. If profits are small, the demand will be small, and the rate of interest will be low; if profits are large, the demand will be large, and the rate of interest will be high.

Relation of profits to interest.

[1] He says it is a great error "to imagine that the rate of interest bears any necessary relation to the quantity or value of money in circulation. An increase in currency has in itself no effect, and is incapable of having any effect, on the rate of interest." *Principles*, vol. i. book iii. ch. xviii. 4. I am aware Mill makes a distinction between money when issued as currency and money when issued as loans, but the question does not affect my argument.

The price of money in new and in old countries.

Money in the United States is more plentiful than it is in England (as proved by the higher prices of commodities and wages in the former than in the latter country), and it is more plentiful in Australia than it is in the United States; but the price of money is lower in England than it is either in the United States or in Australia. The cause of the difference is in the demand; and it is because money can be turned to better account in new than in old countries, that is to say, because it is more useful in the former than in the latter, that there is a greater demand for it, that it commands a higher rate of interest.[1] The low rate of interest prevailing in Holland at the latter end of the seventeenth century was not due to the abundance of capital, although it undoubtedly was abundant enough, but to the absence of profitable means of investment, as every branch of industry had at that period been developed to the utmost. In France and England, on the other hand, the rate of interest was much higher at that time than it was in Holland, for while money could be ordinarily had in Amsterdam, on good mercantile security, at 3½ per cent., the merchants of London had to pay 6 and 7 per cent. for it, and even more.[2] But the high rate ruling in France and England was not due to scarcity of money, but to the fact that

[1] See Hume's *Essays*, p. 177.

[2] Davis, *History of Holland*, iii. p. 243. Childs, *Discovery of Trade*, p. 35.

these countries were then just entering upon a new industrial career, and that they consequently afforded ample means for the profitable investment of capital.[1]

Land is another instrument of production the right to the use of which only is exchanged. Economists generally treat interest as different from rent, interest being regarded as profit on principal, rent as profit on monopoly.[2] There is, however, no essential difference between them. Interest is remuneration for the use of principal; rent is remuneration for the use of principal invested in some kind of property, plus an allowance sufficient to keep the property in repair and ultimately replace it when worn out. Thus understood, the same principle will apply to personal as well as to real property—to steam-engines, ships, machinery, agricultural implements, tools of trade, or household furniture, all of which are let out on hire.

Land.

Land being a monopoly, or limited in quantity, is on that account supposed to be different from personal property, and rent is considered almost exclusively in connection with land. But land is only limited in quantity in the same way as capital or labour is limited, and they are all purchasable and let out for hire in the same way. The wages of labour, the interest on capital, and the rent of land, are all in-

Relation of profits to rent.

[1] McCulloch's *Essays on Economical Policy*, p. 139. McCullaugh's *Industrial History of Free Nations*, vol. ii. p. 363.

[2] Mill, *Principles*, vol. i. book ii. ch. xvi. 1.

fluenced by profits. Why does poor land pay a small rent, or none at all, and rich land a large rent? Obviously because the rich land yields a large profit, and the poor land little or none. It is profit that induces a tenant to give a high rent for good land and a low rent for bad; and it is profit that determines a land-owner not to let his good land for the same rent as his bad, as he knows he can make more out of the former than out of the latter by cultivating it himself. The land which yields no profit pays no rent, and the land which yields the largest profit pays the highest rent. The capitalist who invests his money in land, and the tenant who rents it, both act with a view to profit. The land-owner looks to his rents, the tenant to the income he can make out of the produce of the land during his tenancy; and the amount of capital invested in a property will not determine the rent any more than the rent will determine the price that may be paid for the property. So far from being one of the abstrusest of subjects, as Mill represented it to be, rent is really one of the simplest, when we have once understood the mode in which profit influences demand.

PART III.

RELATIONS.

CHAPTER X.

RELATION TO SOCIOLOGY.

Industrial Science treats of man in his industrial, Sociology in his social, relations. The phenomena of society constitute the subject-matter of the one science, the phenomena of industry the subject-matter of the other. Both are mental sciences, inasmuch as both are concerned with mental forces as the causes of the phenomena which they undertake to investigate. No motives can be said to be exclusively industrial or exclusively social, but as the Egoistic group are the principal causes of industrial phenomena and the Hemeistic of social phenomena, Industrial Science may be said to be primarily concerned with the former, and Sociology with the latter.

Points of agreement between Industrial and Social Science.

There are many other points of agreement between the two sciences. Both treat of man as a member of society. Even the deductionist is bound to acknowledge the social relationship.[1] It would be difficult indeed to

[1] "Political Economy does not treat of the production and distribution of wealth in all states of mankind, but only in what is termed the social state."—*Unsettled Questions*, p. 133.

discover how he could do otherwise, for the existence of property, exchange, and the division of employments, all imply some kind of social sanction or authority. In admitting so much, however, the deductionist is certainly going outside his premisses, for, if a man is incapable of being influenced by other motives than the desire of wealth, he must be destitute of those social qualities which alone can fit him to be a member of society.

The deductionist's hypothesis.

The hypothesis of the deductionist is also open to another objection. His ideal man would not only be unfit for society, but society, as at present constituted, could not exist if his ideal were realized. Society, it is true, is an aggregation of individuals, or units, but for that very reason there could be no society unless there were tendencies in each separate unit towards aggregation. Society, in the essential elements of its character, can never be different from the character of the units of which it is composed. To suppose so would be, as Comte pointed out, as great an error in sociological as it would be in biological reasoning were the biologist to reduce the body chemically into ultimate molecules which have no existence during life. The social affections, the division of functions, the sentiment of authority, and the idea of adjustment, must all find their counterpart in the social unit. No such sentiments, however, are permitted to exist in the ideal of the deductionist. It is in the family that such sentiments have their origin.

The family is the school in which the individual is trained to become a member of society. It is in the family that man comes out of himself, as it were, and lives in another. It is in the family that the first specialization of common functions takes place. It is in the family that the sentiment of authority and the idea of justice have their origin. The social affections are an expansion of the domestic affections; the division of functions in society is an extension of the principle of co-operation which takes place in the family; the parental authority is the basis of authority in the state; and the idea of justice, as embodied in positive law, first finds expression in the adjustment of domestic relations. In primitive times, according to Sir Henry Maine, society did not consist of a collection of individuals, which is the modern conception, but of an aggregation of families. Under the ancient Roman law the parent had absolute control over the persons and property of his children; and the latter were responsible to the paterfamilias, and the paterfamilias was answerable to the state for the defects of his sons. Children were prohibited from holding property apart from their parents, and all their earnings were brought together to the common family stock. And this absolute control by the parent over the persons and property of his family brought with it corresponding responsibilities and duties. The father had to provide for the comfort and well-being of his children; the common fund at his disposal was for their use and benefit, and he had to provide them

The family is the true unit of society.

with the necessaries and conveniences of life in a manner befitting their station in society, to find them the means of employment, and train them to their duties to the state.[1] The individual can only be regarded as a social unit when all his social faculties are fully developed, as they only can be in the domestic circle.

The standpoint of the sociologist.

In investigating the phenomena of industry the standpoint of the economist must be the same as that of the sociologist; that is to say, not the unit, but the aggregate of units, for society only resembles the unit in essential characteristics, not in every particular. One unit differs from another unit, and society consists of various groups of units more or less distinct. According to the extent of its relations or the complexity of its phenomena, society will, therefore, differ from any individual unit or group of units. Thus, what may be to the advantage of a single unit may not be to the advantage of the aggregate of units composing society. The deductionist, however, insists that what is good for one is equally good for all. He views society from the standpoint of the individual, as he understands him, and not from that of society at large. He never attempts to investigate the complex phenomena of society. The social organism as a whole is a matter that forms no part of his inquiry. He begins and ends with the individual. He apparently forgets

[1] *Ancient Law*, p. 125, 3rd edition; see also Niebuhr's *History of Rome*, vol. i. p. 246, English translation.

that his ideal unit has relationship with other units, that these relationships may require adjustment, and that adjustment is only possible when relationships are viewed in the aggregate. When we speak of social or national interests, we mean the interests of the aggregate of units composing the nation, not of the representative unit. When we speak of national wealth we do not mean the wealth of any single unit, or even a group of units, but the aggregate of units of which the nation is made up. One unit does not constitute a nation, and one individual, or even a group of individuals, of enormous wealth does not constitute a wealthy community. Great wealth may coexist with great poverty in a community. The few may be very rich and the great mass very poor at the same time. The Khédive may be said to be the richest potentate in the world, for he owns all the land of Egypt, all the roads, railways, and factories, and has at his command the whole labour of the country; but no one who knows the wretched condition of the great mass of the people in that country would venture to say that Egypt is a wealthy nation. When we come to treat of wealth from the standpoint of society, we are brought face to face with the question of adjustment or distribution, a question which is quite foreign to the premisses of the deductionist, but is inseparable from the consideration both of the family and of society. It is with the production, or rather the accumulation, of wealth that the deductionist really concerns himself, and not its distribution. The desire of wealth as the sole motive would exclude distribution altogether. But the distribution and consumption of wealth belong as much to the phenomena of industry as production or accumulation, and form an integral part of Industrial Science. By narrowing his premisses to acquisition, or the desire of wealth, Mill excludes important elements from the scope of his inquiry. I am aware that in his principal work on Political Economy he includes distribution as well as production, though not consumption; but in this he is scarcely consistent with himself.

Structure of social and industrial life.

The closest relationship is also exhibited in the structure or organization of social and industrial life. As there is a division of functions in society, so there is a division of employments in industry. In the earlier stages of society, and following the type of the family where the paterfamilias had supreme power, the functions of state were performed by one man. He was king, captain, judge, and the regulator of industry. In the more developed stages these various functions were distributed among the more capable members of the community, except industry, which at an early stage became separated from state control.[1] This separation took place in accordance with a natural tendency in society and in order that industry might ascend to the higher stage of the division of employments. To render division of employments possible, an established form of social order was first necessary. Plato says, indeed,

[1] Spencer, *Study of Sociology*, p. 61.

that society was established for this very purpose, for he ascribes the origin of society to the inability of the individual man to supply his own wants."[1] Aristotle implies the same thing when he says that a man who was all-sufficient for his own wants would not associate with other men, and would therefore never become a member of society.[2] Senior takes the same view.[3] Comte goes even further, and speaks of the human race as being bound together by the distribution of their occupations, and of the stability of society as depending on this distribution. "Man," he observes, "can hardly exist in a solitary state: the family can exist in isolation because it can divide its employments, and provide for its wants in a rough kind of way; a spontaneous approximation of families is incessantly exposed to temporary ruptures, occasioned by the most trifling incidents. But when the regular division of employments has spread through any society, the social state begins to acquire a consistency and stability which place it out of danger from particular divergencies."[4]

Subordination of Industrial to Social Science.

On the other hand, the subordination of Industrial to Social Science is indicated by the fact that without the sanction of society there could be no property or wealth, and therefore no incentive to industrial activity. No doubt

[1] *Rep.* ii. ch. 12.

[2] *Politics*, i. 2.

[3] *Political Economy*, p. 75.

[4] *Positive Philosophy*, vol. ii. p. 142, Martineau's translation.

Industrial Science treats of the commercial relations of individuals belonging to different social organizations; but such individuals must always be regarded as members of the community in which the transaction takes place, where they can sue or be sued, as the case may be. Society not only gives its sanction to appropriation, and thereby renders industry possible, but it shows a constant solicitude for the object appropriated. The division of employments necessitates exchange, but there could be no exchange, or, at all events, exchange would be of a very restricted kind, if the state did not enforce contracts, or if it permitted agreements to be broken with impunity. This shows the inseparable connection that exists between Industrial and Social Science.

The application of these principles to Industrial Science will be obvious. The social sympathies are developed through the domestic affections. The sympathies of the individual expand into the family, and from thence into society. Like the force of gravitation, which acts inversely as the square of the distance, the social sympathies are strong or weak in proportion to the nearness or remoteness of the objects. We have greater affection for a near relative than for a stranger; we love our own family more than the particular set with which we associate, our set more than our order, and our order more than society at large.

The Hemeistic or social force is as necessary to industrial life as the Egoistic or personal is to social life. The man who cares only for himself would be as unfit for industrial pursuits as the man who cares only for others would be for society. Both forces being necessary, and both being antagonistic, there comes the question of adjustment. We have already seen how injuriously self-interest operates when left to itself. The effects of the Egoistic force will, however, be counteracted by the Hemeistic. Sympathy will modify selfishness. The social affections will operate as a check upon the egoism of our nature. They will restrain us from doing an injury to others. They will prevent us from seeking our own interest at the expense of our neighbours. They will incite us to acts of benevolence. It is to our sympathetic affections that we owe our charitable institutions, our hospitals, free schools, and our poor laws. The social affections also take the objective form of public opinion, which becomes a sort of unwritten law, imposing its obligations on all classes of society. Praise or dispraise is a powerful incentive to, or restraint upon, action. No one cares to do what public opinion pronounces to be mean, unneighbourly, improper, or contemptible: every one likes to enjoy the good opinion of those with whom he is daily brought into contact, and the respect and esteem of his fellow men.

The sphere of social and industrial forces.

CHAPTER XI.

RELATION TO ETHICS.

Insufficiency of the Hemeistic forces.

We have seen that the self-regarding motives require the aid of the social affections. We shall now endeavour to show that the social affections require the aid of the Ethical Sentiment. With individuals of an unsocial disposition, or those who have little respect for public opinion, the social affections will fail. They will also fail in the case of those who, though they have a certain respect for public opinion, nevertheless think they may avoid its censure for their wrong-doings by escaping detection.

The Lancashire cotton spinners.

The calicoes made in Lancashire for the China and Indian market are known to be of a most inferior quality. The poorer classes in those countries for whom such goods are intended prefer a stiff material, because they believe it indicates strength and durability; and to meet this demand the Lancashire manufacturers, as we have said, supply an article largely adulterated with flour and china clay. The material looks well to the eye of the uninitiated, but the first shower of rain washes out the paste and clay, and the fraudulent nature of the goods is at once exposed. The fear of losing the trade, or what is called enlightened self-interest, has not as yet induced the Lancashire manufacturers to betake themselves to a more honest way of making a living. The subject of adulteration has more than once been discussed before the Manchester Chamber of Commerce, but no resolution condemnatory of the practice has been carried. So long as the present trade is profitable, why should they trouble themselves about the future? The manufacturers probably make more money in one year by selling adulterated goods than they would in ten by selling more honest productions. They may believe that they will lose the trade ultimately, in the same way that the French lost the cloth trade in the Levant in 1837 by similar practices,[1] but that will not influence their conduct in the slightest degree so long as they can secure handsome fortunes in the meantime. Self-interest, therefore, is in favour of the existing system, and the social influences that might operate as a check upon it are all absent in the present instance. The manufacturers never come in contact with their real customers, the people who buy these goods to wear, and the verdict of public opinion in the East, however loudly expressed, would have little or no effect upon the manufacturers living in England. The only public opinion

[1] Say, *Political Economy*, vol. i. ch. xvii.

that would be likely to influence them would be that which finds expression in their own immediate neighbourhood and in their own trade, and that is all in their favour. In such a case as this, therefore, the social affections fail to have any beneficial operation.

In the home trade the social affections fail for a somewhat similar reason. Here, as a rule, a manufacturer sells his goods to wholesale houses or middlemen. The middlemen are his real customers, and between these and the consumers come the retailers, or what is called the trade. The middlemen command the market, for they have the retailers in their hands to a great extent. This naturally gives them immense influence with the manufacturers, who generally make to order such goods as they require, in other words, such as they can easily sell at a handsome profit. It is to the middlemen that most of the modern trade frauds are due. They induce the manufacturers to make a certain standard article of an inferior quality, or put it up in packages short of the usual weight or measurement, "warranted," at the same time, to contain more than they actually do; and as they get the manufacturers to make a corresponding allowance in price, the difference is all clear gain to them, or they share the spoil with the trade.

Manufacturers and middlemen.

A striking illustration of the working of this system is given by Mr. Robert Dale Owen. "When my father," he says, "left me manager of the New Lanark cotton-mills, in the winter of 1824-25, a certain Mr. Bartholomew, who had long been a customer of ours to the extent of twenty-five or thirty thousand dollars a year, came to me one day, asking if I could make him a lot of yarn suitable for ordinary shirting at such a price, naming it. 'We have but one price,' I said, 'and you know well that we sell such yarn 20 per cent. above the rate you propose. 'I know that,' he replied; 'but you *could* make it, so as to be sold at my price.' 'Yes, by using waste and mixing in short-stapled cotton.' 'And it would look almost as well?' 'Perhaps.' 'Then I'll risk it.' 'My father's instructions,' I replied, 'are not to lower the quality of our goods. I'm sorry; but I can't fill your order.' He went off in a huff, but returned two days later. 'See here,' he said, 'don't be Quixotic. I can have the yarn I asked you about spun elsewhere. What's the use of driving a good customer from you? I shall get the stuff I want, and use it, all the same.' 'It would injure the character of our mill.' 'Not if you leave off your trade mark. What do I care about the picture? Mark it as you will.' I hesitated, and finally—not much to my credit—agreed to make the yarn for him. I had it marked with a large B. 'It will stand either for Bartholomew or for *bad*,' I said to him when he came to look at it. 'I'm ashamed to turn such an article out of our mill.' But three weeks later he came again. 'Just the thing!' he said; and he gave me a second order, thrice as large as the first. The B yarn became a popular article in the market, the shirting that was made from it looking smooth, and being sold at some 10 per cent. less than that made from our usual quality. Yet, to my certain knowledge—for I tried it—it did not last half as long as the other. That transaction sits somewhat heavily on my conscience still. Yet it helped to teach me a great lesson. It is my firm belief that, at the present time, purchasers of cotton, woollen, linen, and silk goods, of furniture, hardware, leather goods, and all other manufactured staples, lose, on the average, because of inferior quality, more than half of all the money they pay out."

In such a case as this the manufacturer never comes in contact with the consumers. He never incurs their censure, for the trade mark of his firm is removed. His transactions are with men of the Bartholomew type who take good care to keep their trade secrets to themselves. He simply supplies an article which is "in demand," as the phrase goes, and he flatters himself that there is no deception on his part. If asked about it, he would say that the transaction was perfectly straightforward. He simply supplied an existing demand; this and nothing more. The demand, however, was a fraudulent one, it was supplied with a fraudulent intent, and the consumers were robbed to the extent of the difference in the price between the fraudulent article and the genuine one.

Of course there can be no objection in principle to the law of Correlative Demand so long as the demanders deal equitably the one with the other, and when the contest is not between wants and desires, but between desires and desires, and between wants and wants. Nor can there be any objection to the principle of Competition *per se*, which is simply an assertion of a right to use to one's own advantage the opportunities which circumstances place within one's reach. But it is manifestly objectionable when we exercise that right to the disadvantage of others.

The ancient Greek writers considered Ethics, Social Science or Politics, and what they called Economics, as inseparable. In their estimation these were not distinct sciences, but only branches of the one master science. This master science, according to Plato, was Ethics, and accordingly he commences his *Republic* with a discussion on the subject of Justice, which he regarded as the root of all the virtues and the basis of all good government. With Aristotle, on the other hand, Politics was the master science, because it appropriated all the other sciences to itself.[1] Ethics he considered as the common basis of both Economics and Politics, and Economics he regarded as anterior in point of time to Politics as the οἶκος, or family, existed prior to the πόλις, or state.[2] But however much these writers differed in this respect, they both agreed in regarding the whole group of moral sciences as interdependent and radically one.

Views of Plato and Aristotle.

Modern writers on Ethics and Sociology also acknow-

---

[1] *Ethics*, book i. ch. ii. 3, 4. Aristotle regarded Politics chiefly as an art.

[2] *Economics*, book i. ch. i.

ledge to the fullest extent the interdependence of the moral sciences. They do not pretend to such exactitude in their prevision of phenomena as the economist, or attempt to draw definite lines of demarcation between ethical, social, and economic forces. The moralist does not say, this is an ethical force, that a social, and that an industrial force, and exclude the latter altogether from his consideration. The sociologist does not proceed by separating the social from the ethical and industrial forces, and confine himself strictly to the former. It is only the economist who believes in the doctrine of isolation. He boldly takes his stand on Egoism, pure and simple, and insists on rigorously excluding the Hemeistic and Allostic forces. A little consideration will show, however, that the very foundations of Industrial Science rest on the Ethical Sentiment.

Industry based on the ethical sentiment.

It will not be disputed that industry is based on property. Without property, public or private, there could be no such thing as wealth, and therefore no incentive to production. The desire to appropriate is the primal force of human industry. But this desire, if unrestrained, would only lead to perpetual strife. Each individual would seek to appropriate the appropriations of others as the readiest way of satisfying his desire. No one could be sure of retaining what he had, however acquired, and society, if it existed at all, would be in a continual state of warfare. In order that this desire may find satisfaction, and at the same

Origin of property.

time that the existence of society be rendered possible, property was sanctioned. And its existence is solely due to the Ethical Sentiment. Property is a Right. It is the moral judgment that sanctions its appropriation. The source of this sanction is in man himself, not in the object appropriated. The conflicting claims of individual competitors are adjusted on the ground of equity or justice. The right to hold involves the right to acquire, and as soon as the mind grasped the idea that it was right that the man should retain what he had acquired, the existence of property was possible and not before.

Or we might put the matter in another way. To enjoy without labour is the natural inclination of every man. But the world is so constituted that man cannot enjoy without labour, either on the part of himself or of some one else on his behalf. To procure even the necessaries of life requires the expenditure of human effort, more or less. But no one would care to exert himself unless he were assured that he would enjoy the profits of his exertion. What a man produces or creates he has a right or moral claim to appropriate to his own use.

Appropriation, in the first instance, was no doubt effected by the tribe. In the earliest stages of society the members of a tribe took possession of a certain area of land which they occupied as their hunting ground, and which they held in common against all comers. But even in the rudest state of society the individual was not wholly absorbed in the tribe. Different individuals have different degrees of capacity, and if an individual, while doing his full share of labour in providing for the common wants did something beyond this, justice demanded that he, and not another, should enjoy the fruits of his labour. Hence the origin of private property. Appropriation, public or private, sanctioned by justice, thus became the basis of the whole industrial system.

The Ethical Sentiment is also the basis of contract.

Origin of contract.

A contract, to be valid, must be made with a full knowledge of what it involves; must be voluntary; and there must be an adequate consideration. What does all this mean if it is not another way of saying that a contract to be valid must, in its nature, be equitable and just?

The moral element is, indeed, absolutely essential to

The ethical sentiment necessary.

industry. It is the foundation on which the whole industrial system rests. There would be no production unless the producer had the assurance that he would enjoy the fruits of his labour. The division of employment would not be possible unless the labourer believed that he would obtain a fair price for his products or an adequate remuneration for his services. Commerce could not be carried on unless the contracting parties had faith in each other's honesty, for honesty on the part of the agents is implied in every act of exchange. Honesty, in fact, is an essential attribute of every industrial action. When a man buys anything he mentally asks, Has the seller come honestly by it? is the article what it is represented to be? is the price asked for it a fair one? And it is only when affirmative answers are given to these questions which the intending purchaser puts to himself that any transaction takes place. The moral element is no doubt an embarrassing one for the deductionist to deal with, but if it is essential, its elimination is worse than useless—it is mischievous.

Relation of Industrial to Social and Ethical Science.

Industrial Science is intimately related to Ethics on the one hand, and to Social Science on the other. But it is subordinate to Social Science as the latter is again subordinate to Ethics. Social Science is the key-stone of the arch of which Ethics is the foundation. It is the Social Sanction that gives expression and force to the Ethical Sentiment, and it is to the Ethical Sentiment that we owe the ideas of property and contract. There could be no contract without exchange, no exchange without property, or something to exchange, and there could be no property unless society sanctioned appropriation. Thus Ethics, Sociology, and Industrial Science are not separate and independent, but inseparable and interdependent sciences, each being necessary to the other, each forming a part of one whole Science of Man.

CHAPTER XII.

RELATION TO ART.

Science and art.

THE difference between science and art may be explained in a few words. Science investigates, art applies. Science deals with what is, art with what should be. Science treats of phenomena, and the causes or forces which produce them; art employs these forces to produce phenomena of the same or of a different kind, according to the aim of the artist.

The art of legislation.

As there is an art and a science of ethics, and an art and a science of society, so there is an art and a science of industry. The art of industry is Industrial Legislation. Positive law stands in the same relation to natural law that art does to science. Like true art, wise legislation is based on scientific law. The legislator makes use of the facts of Industrial Science, but he does not confine himself to these; he also uses the materials furnished him by the moralist and sociologist, in the same way as the navigator does with the facts of astronomy and geometry, as the agriculturist with those of chemistry, physiology, and botany, or as the doctor with those of anatomy, physiology, and pathology.

The Art of Political Economy is entirely ignored by the modern school of economists, but not because they modestly believe that the facts of their science are not sufficiently established to be made available for the purposes of art, but because they think its principles, or laws, as they are pleased to call them, are naturally adapted to every condition of economic existence. What in other departments of knowledge would be termed rules of art, are with them designated scientific laws. They have laws for everything, but whether they are laws in the strictly scientific sense may be a matter of dispute. We hear of the Laws of Production, the Laws of Demand and Supply, the Laws of Value, the Laws of Price, even the Laws of Free Trade, and how many more beside it would be difficult to say, for the bare enumeration of them would fill a good-sized volume. But the great majority of these so-called laws are mere truisms. Even the fundamental maxim of this school, that mankind desire to obtain the greatest amount of wealth with the least expenditure of labour or self-sacrifice, is a mere truism, on a par with such maxims as these, that a man will choose the greater of two goods, that of two evils he will choose the lesser, or that of two roads to the same place he will take the shortest. All these and similar platitudes imply nothing more than average intelligence on the part of the agents.

Industrial art ignored in modern Political Economy.

We have seen that Industrial Science has to deal

with mental forces. The laws of the science will therefore be formulated statements of the modes in which these forces operate. Mental forces are of two kinds, psychological and moral. The laws of psychological forces are few and simple. They are those of Contiguity, of Similarity, and of Compound Association. But of the moral laws, the laws of human action, what do we really know about them? We know, indeed, that mankind act from motives, and we can enumerate many of such motives, and we know generally the kind of actions which certain motives influence. We know also that some motives are more powerful than others, judging by their effects; that the Hemeistic, for instance, are stronger than the Allostic, and that the Egoistic are stronger than either; but motives vary in strength, or, what amounts to the same thing, the receptiveness of the agent varies with times and circumstances, so that the same motive which will determine action at one time, or under one set of conditions, will not at another time, or under another set of conditions. If we take a given motive and isolate it from all others, we may certainly be able to ascertain approximately how the agent will act under its influence. We say "approximately" only, for as we can never know the strength of a motive but by its results, so we can never previse its precise operation. But in actual life a motive is never isolated in this way. There are always several motives operating concurrently on the mind, some of which determine action and others not,

Mental phenomena incapable of prevision.

and we can never tell beforehand which will prevail. We can never measure the strength of a motive quantitatively, and we can therefore never previse its effect on the volition. No doubt when several motives have the same general tendency we may be able to tell pretty accurately the result, just as we can in the case of an isolated motive; but when they are in conflict we can never predicate which will get the mastery, and even if we could, we cannot tell the exact amount of deflection which may result from the subjected motives. A man is both hungry and fatigued at the same time. The one state predisposes him to exertion, the other to rest, and the result will prove whether the desire to eat or the desire to rest was the stronger motive and which the weaker, and possibly also the influence of the latter on the former; but it would have been impossible to previse the result. Even if we are to take a purely hedonistic view of human nature we would still be no nearer prevision, as pains and pleasures are presented to the human mind in such a variety of aspects that it can never be said, absolutely, that mankind always act so as to avert the one or secure the greatest amount of the other.

But it does not follow there is no Moral Science.

It does not follow, however, that because there can be no prevision there can be no science. We cannot previse geological phenomena, and yet it will not be disputed that there is a Science of Geology. The various processes of upheaval, denudation, and subsidence, take place according to certain general laws which are more or less understood, but we cannot foretell their effects, as they vary according to the nature and strength of the subterranean forces which cannot be measured quantitatively. Even in Biology and Psychology, as Mr. Herbert Spencer has observed, the previsions are, most of them, only qualificative, and even when they are quantitative, their quantitativeness can only be ascertained approximately.[1] In Psychology, Ethics, Sociology, and Industrial Science, the phenomena are only qualificative, and are therefore altogether incapable of exact prevision.

The deductionists insist on prevision.

Nothing but exact prevision will, however, satisfy the deductionists. With them, Political Economy is an exact science or it is nothing; and in order to make it exact they isolate it from the other moral sciences. They adopt an arbitrary conception of man, assume him to be impelled by a single motive, and then they proceed to explain how he must necessarily act under its influence. And no sooner have they adopted this assumption than they proceed to dogmatize upon it as if it were no assumption at all. They make believe, in fact, that they have not assumed anything, and present their deductions as if they were absolute, incontrovertible truths, and all this they do with such an air of infallibility as would be ridiculous were it not mischievous.

But this only leads them further astray. So satisfied

---

[1] *Sociology*, p. 45.

are they with the manner in which they have elaborated their system, that they have come to believe in its absolute perfectibility. So admirably adapted, in their opinion, are the laws of their science to meet every industrial requirement, that they imagine nothing more is necessary than that they should be left to their free operation. Borrowing a shibboleth from certain French traders, they preach henceforth the gospel of *laissez faire*. To make any attempt to promote industry, either directly or indirectly, was naturally enough regarded by the commercial mind in Colbert's day as an interference with vested interests; but by the economist of the modern English school such an attempt is looked upon as nothing less than a gross violation of the first principles of economic law, an unwarrantable outrage on the established order of nature. "Free exchange," we are told by one of that school, "between man and man—or, what is the same thing, free trade—is action in accordance with the teachings of nature. Protection, on the other hand, is an attempt to make things better than nature made them."[1] To all such objections I would only reply that it is the function of art to improve upon nature, or, to use the words of Polixenes to Perdita—

Laissez faire.

> "This is an art
> Which does mend nature,—change it rather: but
> The art itself is nature."

---

[1] Mr. David Wells in *The Atlantic Monthly* for August, 1875.

The gardener mends nature when he gives variety of tone and colour to the landscape. The agriculturist mends nature when he drains his land, when he adds any ingredients to the soil to increase its fertility, and when he improves the quality of his seed or his breed of live stock. In the same manner a legislature mends nature when it passes a measure for the removal of nuisances which are injurious to health, promotes education, or provides for the administration of justice. Every act of administration on the part of the state is an interference with nature: every positive law is an interference with natural law. Is there anything peculiarly sacred about industry that it should be looked upon as sacrilege to lay hands on it? The question does not require a moment's serious consideration. The dogma of *laissez faire*, if applied to social life, would be the negation of all law.

State interference necessary.

The state ever has interfered, and we venture to say, ever will interfere with industry, for the simple reason that it cannot help doing so. For what purpose, if not in the interests of industry, does the state protect property, enforce contracts, and punish fraud? If we examine the statute books of any civilized people, we shall find the greater portion of them occupied with laws which, either directly or indirectly, affect trade. Indeed, the number of laws of this description in any country is a certain criterion of its industrial development. In the earlier stages of society, when industry was of the rudest kind, the number of laws relating to trade were few and simple. According to Sir Henry Maine, the only form of dishonesty treated of in the most ancient Roman law was theft;[1] but as trade extended the opportunities for fraud were increased, and the laws for its repression were increased in proportion. The history of the acts passed by our own legislature shows very clearly that legislation followed crime, and crime followed industry. Laws relating to the tenure and transfer of land occupied an early place in the statute book, for land is generally the first thing appropriated. With the development of trade there followed the laws relating to guilds and apprenticeships; as competition increased between people in the same occupation, bringing in its train new kinds of fraud, we have laws for the suppression of adulteration and against the use of light weights and short measures; as commerce extended, we have laws for regulating shipping, banks, insurance companies, and institutions of a like character; and with the introduction of the factory system we have laws innumerable for the regulation of the hours of labour, and generally for the protection of women and young persons in factories.

Legislative art follows nature's method.

But while art mends, it also follows nature. It not only works in accordance with nature's law, but it follows nature's method. Nature does not lay down a law and expect it to be observed as a matter of course. She attaches a penalty to

---

[1] *Ancient Law*, p. 307.

the breach of it, and so presents a motive for its observance. If I put my finger over a flame, I suffer pain; if I go without food, I feel hungry; if I eat or drink too much, I have an uneasy sensation of repletion. The penalty attached to the breach of a law acts as a deterrent. The legislator follow nature's method in this respect. He attaches a penalty to every breach of the law in order to ensure its observance, and this acts as a deterrent on the human mind. A good or a bad action is performed because there is a motive for its performance. To prevent the performance of a bad action, a stronger counteracting motive must be supplied. A man may have a strong motive to steal, but if the penalty for stealing be imprisonment with hard labour for a term of years, this will usually form a stronger motive than the desire to appropriate, and will therefore counteract it.

Ends and means of art.

Art has to do with ends and means. Not only must the legislator have a proper object in view in framing a law, but he must take the proper means to attain that object. The means at his command are motives which must be capable of influencing the human mind. If adequate motives are presented, the law will be successful in its operation; if inadequate, it will fail. All that science demands of art is the presentation of adequate motives.

Social ends.

Is it desirable, from an individual point of view, that a certain act should be performed? Then the individual should perform it. Is it desirable, from a social point of view, that a certain act should be performed? Then the state should perform it. It would be absurd to expect society to do for the individual what is chiefly for the individual's advantage; and it would be equally absurd to expect the individual to do for society what is chiefly for the interest of society. If society has no ends in view, then social organization will be reduced to a nullity; if it has ends, then it must take the proper means to accomplish those ends.

Social means.

What is good for all, and not merely for an individual or a class, should be undertaken by the state; what benefits only the few should be left to private enterprise. Is it good for the whole community that there should be ships and commerce? Then the state should make harbours and build lighthouses. Is it good for the whole community that there should be intercommunication between the various parts of the country? Then the state should make roads or build railways, or sanction and promote their being made. Is it good for the whole community that the population should be fully employed and adequately remunerated? Then it may be necessary for the state to promote, by such means as it has in its power, the growth of manufactures. This is rank heresy, I know, but the fact that it is so will not invalidate my argument in the slightest degree. The interests of the individual are sometimes antagonistic to, more often identical with, those of society, but they can never be coextensive with them. The individual is not expected to sacrifice himself for the benefit of society, but it is expected of society, as it is of the individual, that it will look after its own interests. The principle laid down by Mill, that state interference is justifiable when important public services are to be performed which there is no individual specially interested in performing, nor any adequate remuneration which would naturally or spontaneously attend their performance, holds good in all cases.[1]

One cause of industrial supremacy.

Mill makes the pregnant remark that "the superiority of one country over another in a branch of production often arises only from having begun it sooner."[2] To give a country this start may, under certain circumstances, be a public benefit, and therefore a public duty. To do so no doubt may entail a little temporary self-sacrifice on the part of the public, but this should not be considered a very serious objection. Success in anything is always attended with more or less sacrifice at the start. We must plant a tree before we can enjoy its fruit; we must build our houses before we can live in them. This kind of sacrifice is entailed on individuals equally with society. To establish a business, some expenditure of time, labour, and money is required; to learn a trade, one must serve a long apprenticeship; to acquire a profession, a youth must not only give years of service gratuitously, but often a bonus as well. The same principle is acted on by corporations as well as

[1] *Principles*, vol. ii. book v. ch. xi. 15.

[2] *Ibid*, vol. ii. book v. ch. x. 1.

by individuals. The inhabitants of a district believe that the establishment of a certain branch of manufacture would be beneficial to them, and they offer certain advantages to capitalists to embark in the enterprise—just as was done by the citizens of Amsterdam with the view of inducing the employers and artisans of Aix to settle in their city—and no one doubts the propriety of the proceeding. The ratepayers of a town want a good harbour, and they impose a temporary rate on themselves for the purpose of raising the necessary funds—in the same way as the ratepayers of Greenock did in order to secure the West India sugar trade—and they are everywhere applauded for their energy and enterprise. Why should that which is proper for the individual or corporation to do, be improper for the state?

Buying in the cheapest market.

By the modern school of economists it is considered a wise policy to import commodities from those places where they can be purchased cheapest. But why should it not be considered an equally wise policy to have commodities produced in those places where the cost of production would be least? Why should we not ascertain the countries where the raw material can be obtained most abundantly, and carry thither our capital and labour;[1] or, having the raw material in abundance, why not import the labour to manufacture it? It was in this manner

[1] This view is put by Mill as an argument in favour of state-assisted emigration.—*Principles*, vol. ii. book v. ch. xi. 14.

that England established her woollen manufactures. Instead of exporting her raw wool, and reimporting it again when manufactured, she kept her wool and imported skilled workmen from Holland to make it into cloth.

Society the best judge of its own interests.

The Economists insist that the individual is the best judge of his own interests. The dictum is one that I am not disposed to dispute. On the contrary, I accept it without the slightest hesitation. All that I insist upon is that the principle should have a more general application, and that society should, in respect to ability of judging as to its own interests, be put upon the same footing as the individual.

INDEX OF SUBJECTS.

A.

B.

C.

D.

E.

J.

L.

M.

N.

O.

P.

Q.

R.

S.

T.

U.

V.

W.

CAXTON PRINTING WORKS, BECCLES.

CATALOGUE

OF

PRACTICAL AND SCIENTIFIC BOOKS

PUBLISHED BY

HENRY CAREY BAIRD & CO.,

INDUSTRIAL PUBLISHERS, BOOKSELLERS AND IMPORTERS,

810 WALNUT STREET,
PHILADELPHIA.

☞ Any of the Books comprised in this Catalogue will be sent free of postage at the printed prices to any address in the World.

☞ A Descriptive Catalogue, 96 pages, 8vo., and our other Catalogues, the whole covering all of the branches of Science Applied to the Arts, sent free and free of postage to any one in any part of the world, who will furnish us with his address.

☞ Where not otherwise stated, all of the Books in this Catalogue are bound in muslin.

CATALOGUE
OF
Practical and Scientific Books
PUBLISHED BY
HENRY CAREY BAIRD & CO.
INDUSTRIAL PUBLISHERS, BOOKSELLERS AND IMPORTERS,
810 Walnut Street, Philadelphia.

☞ Any of the Books comprised in this Catalogue will be sent by mail, free of postage, to any address in the world, at the publication prices.

☞ A Descriptive Catalogue, 96 pages, 8vo., will be sent free and free of postage, to any one in any part of the world, who will furnish his address.

☞ Where not otherwise stated, all of the Books in this Catalogue are bound in muslin.

AMATEUR MECHANICS' WORKSHOP:
A treatise containing plain and concise directions for the manipulation of Wood and Metals, including Casting, Forging, Brazing, Soldering and Carpentry. By the author of the "Lathe and Its Uses." Third edition. Illustrated. 8vo. $3.00

ANDRES.—A Practical Treatise on the Fabrication of Volatile and Fat Varnishes, Lacquers, Siccatives and Sealing Waxes.
From the German of ERWIN ANDRES, Manufacturer of Varnishes and Lacquers. With additions on the Manufacture and Application of Varnishes, Stains for Wood, Horn, Ivory, Bone and Leather. From the German of DR. EMIL WINCKLER and LOUIS E. ANDES. The whole translated and edited by WILLIAM T. BRANNT. With 11 illustrations. 12mo. $2.50

ARLOT.—A Complete Guide for Coach Painters:
Translated from the French of M. ARLOT, Coach Painter; for eleven years Foreman of Painting to M. Eherler, Coach Maker, Paris. By A. A. FESQUET, Chemist and Engineer. To which is added an Appendix, containing Information respecting the Materials and the Practice of Coach and Car Painting and Varnishing in the United States and Great Britain. 12mo. $1.25

ARMENGAUD, AMOROUX, AND JOHNSON.—The Practical Draughtsman's Book of Industrial Design, and Machinist's and Engineer's Drawing Companion:

Forming a Complete Course of Mechanical Engineering and Architectural Drawing. From the French of M. Armengaud the elder, Prof. of Design in the Conservatoire of Arts and Industry, Paris, and MM. Armengaud the younger, and Amoroux, Civil Engineers. Rewritten and arranged with additional matter and plates, selections from and examples of the most useful and generally employed mechanism of the day. By WILLIAM JOHNSON, Assoc. Inst. C. E. Illustrated by fifty folio steel plates, and fifty wood-cuts. A new edition, 4to., half morocco $10.00

ARMSTRONG.—The Construction and Management of Steam Boilers:

By R. ARMSTRONG, C. E. With an Appendix by ROBERT MALLET, C. E., F. R. S. Seventh Edition. Illustrated. 1 vol. 12mo. 75

ARROWSMITH.—Paper-Hanger's Companion:

A Treatise in which the Practical Operations of the Trade are Systematically laid down: with Copious Directions Preparatory to Papering; Preventives against the Effect of Damp on Walls; the various Cements and Pastes Adapted to the Several Purposes of the Trade; Observations and Directions for the Panelling and Ornamenting of Rooms, etc. By JAMES ARROWSMITH. 12mo., cloth $1.25

ASHTON.—The Theory and Practice of the Art of Designing Fancy Cotton and Woollen Cloths from Sample:

Giving full instructions for reducing drafts, as well as the methods of spooling and making out harness for cross drafts and finding any required reed; with calculations and tables of yarn. By FREDERIC T. ASHTON, Designer, West Pittsfield, Mass. With fifty-two illustrations. One vol. folio $10.00

AUERBACH—CROOKES.—Anthracen:

Its Constitution, Properties, Manufacture and Derivatives, including Artificial Alizarin, Anthrapurpurin, etc., with their applications in Dyeing and Printing. By G. AUERBACH. Translated and edited from the revised manuscript of the Author, by WM. CROOKES, F. R. S., Vice-President of the Chemical Society. 8vo. . . $5.00

BAIRD.—Miscellaneous Papers on Economic Questions. By Henry Carey Baird. (*In preparation.*)

BAIRD.—The American Cotton Spinner, and Manager's and Carder's Guide:

A Practical Treatise on Cotton Spinning; giving the Dimensions and Speed of Machinery, Draught and Twist Calculations, etc.; with notices of recent Improvements: together with Rules and Examples for making changes in the sizes and numbers of Roving and Yarn. Compiled from the papers of the late ROBERT H. BAIRD. 12mo. $1.50

BAIRD.—Standard Wages Computing Tables:
An Improvement in all former Methods of Computation, so arranged that wages for days, hours, or fractions of hours, at a specified rate per day or hour, may be ascertained at a glance. By T. SPANGLER BAIRD. Oblong folio $5.00

BAKER.—Long-Span Railway Bridges:
Comprising Investigations of the Comparative Theoretical and Practical Advantages of the various Adopted or Proposed Type Systems of Construction; with numerous Formulæ and Tables. By B. BAKER. 12mo. $1.50

BAKER.—The Mathematical Theory of the Steam-Engine:
With Rules at length, and Examples worked out for the use of Practical Men. By T. BAKER, C. E., with numerous Diagrams. Sixth Edition, Revised by Prof. J. R. YOUNG. 12mo. . 75

BARLOW.—The History and Principles of Weaving, by Hand and by Power:
Reprinted, with Considerable Additions, from "Engineering," with a chapter on Lace-making Machinery, reprinted from the Journal of the "Society of Arts." By ALFRED BARLOW. With several hundred illustrations. 8vo., 443 pages $10.00

BARR.—A Practical Treatise on the Combustion of Coal:
Including descriptions of various mechanical devices for the Economic Generation of Heat by the Combustion of Fuel, whether solid, liquid or gaseous. 8vo. $2.50

BARR.—A Practical Treatise on High Pressure Steam Boilers:
Including Results of Recent Experimental Tests of Boiler Materials, together with a Description of Approved Safety Apparatus, Steam Pumps, Injectors and Economizers in actual use. By WM. M. BARR. 204 Illustrations. 8vo. $3.00

BAUERMAN.—A Treatise on the Metallurgy of Iron:
Containing Outlines of the History of Iron Manufacture, Methods of Assay, and Analysis of Iron Ores, Processes of Manufacture of Iron and Steel, etc., etc. By H. BAUERMAN, F. G. S., Associate of the Royal School of Mines. Fifth Edition, Revised and Enlarged. Illustrated with numerous Wood Engravings from Drawings by J. B. JORDAN. 12mo. $2.00

BAYLES.—House Drainage and Water Service:
In Cities, Villages and Rural Neighborhoods. With Incidental Consideration of Certain Causes Affecting the Healthfulness of Dwellings. By JAMES C. BAYLES, Editor of "The Iron Age" and "The Metal Worker." With numerous illustrations. 8vo. cloth, $3.00

BEANS.—A Treatise on Railway Curves and Location of Railroads:
By E. W. BEANS, C. E. Illustrated. 12mo. Tucks . $1.50

BECKETT.—A Rudimentary Treatise on Clocks, and Watches and Bells:
By Sir EDMUND BECKETT, Bart., LL. D., Q. C. F. R. A. S. With numerous illustrations. Seventh Edition, Revised and Enlarged. 12mo. $2.25

BELL.—Carpentry Made Easy:
Or, The Science and Art of Framing on a New and Improved System. With Specific Instructions for Building Balloon Frames, Barn Frames, Mill Frames, Warehouses, Church Spires, etc. Comprising also a System of Bridge Building, with Bills, Estimates of Cost, and valuable Tables. Illustrated by forty-four plates, comprising nearly 200 figures. By WILLIAM E. BELL, Architect and Practical Builder. 8vo. $5.00

BEMROSE.—Fret-Cutting and Perforated Carving:
With fifty-three practical illustrations. By W. BEMROSE, JR. 1 vol. quarto $3.00

BEMROSE.—Manual of Buhl-work and Marquetry:
With Practical Instructions for Learners, and ninety colored designs. By W. BEMROSE, JR. 1 vol. quarto $3.00

BEMROSE.—Manual of Wood Carving:
With Practical Illustrations for Learners of the Art, and Original and Selected Designs. By WILLIAM BEMROSE, JR. With an Introduction by LLEWELLYN JEWITT, F. S. A., etc. With 128 illustrations, 4to. $3.00

BILLINGS.—Tobacco:
Its History, Variety, Culture, Manufacture, Commerce, and Various Modes of Use. By E. R. BILLINGS. Illustrated by nearly 200 engravings. 8vo. $3.00

BIRD.—The American Practical Dyers' Companion:
Comprising a Description of the Principal Dye-Stuffs and Chemicals used in Dyeing, their Natures and Uses; Mordants, and How Made; with the best American, English, French and German processes for Bleaching and Dyeing Silk, Wool, Cotton, Linen, Flannel, Felt, Dress Goods, Mixed and Hosiery Yarns, Feathers, Grass, Felt, Fur, Wool, and Straw Hats, Jute Yarn, Vegetable Ivory, Mats, Skins, Furs, Leather, etc., etc. By Wood, Aniline, and other Processes, together with Remarks on Finishing Agents, and Instructions in the Finishing of Fabrics, Substitutes for Indigo, Water-Proofing of Materials, Tests and Purification of Water, Manufacture of Aniline and other New Dye Wares, Harmonizing Colors, etc., etc.; embracing in all over 800 Receipts for Colors and Shades, *accompanied by* 170 *Dyed Samples of Raw Materials and Fabrics*. By F. J. BIRD, Practical Dyer, Author of "The Dyers' Hand-Book." 8vo. $10.00

BLENKARN.—Practical Specifications of Works executed in Architecture, Civil and Mechanical Engineering, and in Road Making and Sewering:
To which are added a series of practically useful Agreements and Reports. By JOHN BLENKARN. Illustrated by fifteen large folding plates. 8vo. $9.00

BLINN.—A Practical Workshop Companion for Tin, Sheet-Iron, and Copper-plate Workers:
Containing Rules for describing various kinds of Patterns used by Tin, Sheet-Iron and Copper-plate Workers; Practical Geometry;

Mensuration of Surfaces and Solids; Tables of the Weights of Metals, Lead-pipe, etc.; Tables of Areas and Circumferences of Circles; Japan, Varnishes, Lackers, Cements, Compositions, etc., etc. By LEROY J. BLINN, Master Mechanic. With over One Hundred Illustrations. 12mo. $2.50

BOOTH.—Marble Worker's Manual:

Containing Practical Information respecting Marbles in general, their Cutting, Working and Polishing; Veneering of Marble; Mosaics; Composition and Use of Artificial Marble, Stuccos, Cements, Receipts, Secrets, etc., etc. Translated from the French by M. L. BOOTH. With an Appendix concerning American Marbles. 12mo., cloth $1.50

BOOTH and MORFIT.—The Encyclopædia of Chemistry, Practical and Theoretical:

Embracing its application to the Arts, Metallurgy, Mineralogy, Geology, Medicine and Pharmacy. By JAMES C. BOOTH, Melter and Refiner in the United States Mint, Professor of Applied Chemistry in the Franklin Institute, etc., assisted by CAMPBELL MORFIT, author of "Chemical Manipulations," etc. Seventh Edition. Complete in one volume, royal 8vo., 978 pages, with numerous wood-cuts and other illustrations $5.00

BRAMWELL.—The Wool Carder's Vade-Mecum:

A Complete Manual of the Art of Carding Textile Fabrics. By W. C. BRAMWELL. Third Edition, revised and enlarged. Illustrated. pp. 400. 12mo. $2.50

BRANNT.—The Techno-Chemical Receipt Book:

Containing several thousand Receipts comprising the latest and most useful discoveries in Chemical Technology and Industry. Edited from the German of DRS. E. WINCKLER, HEINTZE and MIERZINSKI, with additions by W. T. BRANNT. (*In preparation.*)

BROWN.—Five Hundred and Seven Mechanical Movements:

Embracing all those which are most important in Dynamics, Hydraulics, Hydrostatics, Pneumatics, Steam-Engines, Mill and other Gearing, Presses, Horology and Miscellaneous Machinery; and including many movements never before published, and several of which have only recently come into use. By HENRY T. BROWN. 12mo. $1.00

BUCKMASTER.—The Elements of Mechanical Physics:

By J. C. BUCKMASTER. Illustrated with numerous engravings. 12mo. $1.50

BULLOCK.—The American Cottage Builder:

A Series of Designs, Plans and Specifications, from $200 to $20,000, for Homes for the People; together with Warming, Ventilation, Drainage, Painting and Landscape Gardening. By JOHN BULLOCK, Architect and Editor of "The Rudiments of Architecture and Building," etc., etc. Illustrated by 75 engravings. 8vo. $3.50

BULLOCK.—The Rudiments of Architecture and Building:

For the use of Architects, Builders, Draughtsmen, Machinists, Engineers and Mechanics. Edited by JOHN BULLOCK, author of "The American Cottage Builder." Illustrated by 250 Engravings. 8vo. $3.50

BURGH.—Practical Rules for the Proportions of Modern Engines and Boilers for Land and Marine Purposes.

By N. P. BURGH, Engineer. 12mo. $1.50

BURNS.—The American Woolen Manufacturer:

A Practical Treatise on the Manufacture of Woolens, in two parts. Part First gives full and explicit instructions upon Drafting, Cross-Drawing, Combining Weaves, and the correct arrangement of Weights, Colors and Sizes of Yarns to produce any desired fabric. Illustrated with diagrams of various weavings, and twelve samples of cloth for explanation and practice. Part Second is fully supplied with extended Tables, Rules, Examples, Explanations, etc.; gives full and practical information, in detailed order, from the stock department to the market, of the proper selection and use of the various grades and staples of wool, with the admixture of waste, cotton and shoddy; and the proper application and economical use of the various oils, drugs, dye stuffs, soaps, belting, etc. Also, the most approved method for Calculating and Estimating the Cost of Goods, for all Wool, Wool Waste and Cotton and Cotton Warps. With Examples and Calculations on the Circular motions of Wheels, Pinions, Drums, Pulleys and Gears, how to speed them, etc. The two parts combined form a whole work on the American way of manufacturing more complete than any yet issued. By GEORGE C. BURNS. 8vo. . . $6.50

BYLES.—Sophisms of Free Trade and Popular Political Economy Examined.

By a BARRISTER (SIR JOHN BARNARD BYLES, Judge of Common Pleas). From the Ninth English Edition, as published by the Manchester Reciprocity Association. 12mo. . . . $1.25

BYRN.—The Complete Practical Brewer:

Or Plain, Accurate and Thorough Instructions in the Art of Brewing Beer, Ale, Porter, including the Process of Making Bavarian Beer, all the Small Beers, such as Root-beer, Ginger-pop, Sarsaparilla-beer, Mead, Spruce Beer, etc. Adapted to the use of Public Brewers and Private Families. By M. LA FAYETTE BYRN, M. D. With illustrations. 12mo. . . . .

BYRN.—The Complete Practical Distiller:

Comprising the most perfect and exact Theoretical and Practical Description of the Art of Distillation and Rectification; including all of the most recent improvements in distilling apparatus; instructions for preparing spirits from the numerous vegetables, fruits, etc; directions for the distillation and preparation of all kinds of brandies and other spirits, spirituous and other compounds, etc. By M. LA FAYETTE BYRN, M. D. Eighth Edition. To which are added Practical Directions for Distilling, from the French of Th. Fling, Brewer and Distiller. 12mo. $1.50

BYRNE.—Hand-Book for the Artisan, Mechanic, and Engineer:

Comprising the Grinding and Sharpening of Cutting Tools, Abrasive Processes, Lapidary Work, Gem and Glass Engraving, Varnishing and Lackering, Apparatus, Materials and Processes for Grinding and

Polishing, etc. By OLIVER BYRNE. Illustrated by 185 wood engravings. 8vo. $5.00

BYRNE.—Pocket-Book for Railroad and Civil Engineers:
Containing New, Exact and Concise Methods for Laying out Railroad Curves, Switches, Frog Angles and Crossings; the Staking out of work; Levelling; the Calculation of Cuttings; Embankments; Earthwork, etc. By OLIVER BYRNE. 18mo., full bound, pocket-book form $1.75

BYRNE.—The Practical Metal-Worker's Assistant:
Comprising Metallurgic Chemistry; the Arts of Working all Metals and Alloys; Forging of Iron and Steel; Hardening and Tempering; Melting and Mixing; Casting and Founding; Works in Sheet Metal; the Processes Dependent on the Ductility of the Metals; Soldering; and the most Improved Processes and Tools employed by Metal-Workers. With the Application of the Art of Electro-Metallurgy to Manufacturing Processes; collected from Original Sources, and from the works of Holtzapffel, Bergeron, Leupold, Plumier, Napier, Scoffern, Clay, Fairbairn and others. By OLIVER BYRNE. A new, revised and improved edition, to which is added an Appendix, containing The Manufacture of Russian Sheet-Iron. By JOHN PERCY, M. D., F. R. S. The Manufacture of Malleable Iron Castings, and Improvements in Bessemer Steel. By A. A. FESQUET, Chemist and Engineer. With over Six Hundred Engravings, Illustrating every Branch of the Subject. 8vo. $7.00

BYRNE.—The Practical Model Calculator:
For the Engineer, Mechanic, Manufacturer of Engine Work, Naval Architect, Miner and Millwright. By OLIVER BYRNE. 8vo., nearly 600 pages $4.50

CABINET MAKER'S ALBUM OF FURNITURE:
Comprising a Collection of Designs for various Styles of Furniture. Illustrated by Forty-eight Large and Beautifully Engraved Plates. Oblong, 8vo. $3.50

CALLINGHAM.—Sign Writing and Glass Embossing:
A Complete Practical Illustrated Manual of the Art. By JAMES CALLINGHAM. 12mo. $1.50

CAMPIN.—A Practical Treatise on Mechanical Engineering:
Comprising Metallurgy, Moulding, Casting, Forging, Tools, Workshop Machinery, Mechanical Manipulation, Manufacture of Steam-Engines, etc. With an Appendix on the Analysis of Iron and Iron Ores. By FRANCIS CAMPIN, C. E. To which are added, Observations on the Construction of Steam Boilers, and Remarks upon Furnaces used for Smoke Prevention; with a Chapter on Explosions. By R. ARMSTRONG, C. E., and JOHN BOURNE. Rules for Calculating the Change Wheels for Screws on a Turning Lathe, and for a Wheel-cutting Machine. By J. LA NICCA. Management of Steel, Including Forging, Hardening, Tempering, Annealing, Shrinking and Expansion; and the Case-hardening of Iron. By G. EDE. 8vo. Illustrated with twenty-nine plates and 100 wood engravings $5.00

CAREY.—A Memoir of Henry C. Carey.
By DR. WM. ELDER. With a portrait. 8vo., cloth . . 75

CAREY.—The Works of Henry C. Carey:
Harmony of Interests: Agricultural, Manufacturing and Commercial. 8vo. $1.50
Manual of Social Science. Condensed from Carey's "Principles of Social Science." By KATE MCKEAN. 1 vol. 12mo. . $2.25
Miscellaneous Works. With a Portrait. 2 vols. 8vo. $6.00
Past, Present and Future. 8vo. $2.50
Principles of Social Science. 3 volumes, 8vo. . . $10.00
The Slave-Trade, Domestic and Foreign; Why it Exists, and How it may be Extinguished (1853). 8vo. $2.00
The Unity of Law: As Exhibited in the Relations of Physical, Social, Mental and Moral Science (1872). 8vo. . . $3.50

CLARK.—Tramways, their Construction and Working:
Embracing a Comprehensive History of the System. With an exhaustive analysis of the various modes of traction, including horse-power, steam, heated water and compressed air; a description of the varieties of Rolling stock, and ample details of cost and working expenses. By D. KINNEAR CLARK. Illustrated by over 200 wood engravings, and thirteen folding plates. 2 vols. 8vo. . $12.50

COLBURN.—The Locomotive Engine:
Including a Description of its Structure, Rules for Estimating its Capabilities, and Practical Observations on its Construction and Management. By ZERAH COLBURN. Illustrated. 12mo. . $1.00

COLLENS.—The Eden of Labor; or, the Christian Utopia.
By T. WHARTON COLLENS, author of "Humanics," "The History of Charity," etc. 12mo. Paper cover, $1.00; Cloth . $1.25

COOLEY.—A Complete Practical Treatise on Perfumery:
Being a Hand-book of Perfumes, Cosmetics and other Toilet Articles. With a Comprehensive Collection of Formulæ. By ARNOLD J. COOLEY. 12mo. $1.50

COOPER.—A Treatise on the use of Belting for the Transmission of Power.
With numerous illustrations of approved and actual methods of arranging Main Driving and Quarter Twist Belts, and of Belt Fastenings. Examples and Rules in great number for exhibiting and calculating the size and driving power of Belts. Plain, Particular and Practical Directions for the Treatment, Care and Management of Belts. Descriptions of many varieties of Beltings, together with chapters on the Transmission of Power by Ropes; by Iron and Wood Frictional Gearing; on the Strength of Belting Leather; and on the Experimental Investigations of Morin, Briggs, and others. By JOHN H. COOPER, M. E. 8vo. $3.50

CRAIK.—The Practical American Millwright and Miller.
By DAVID CRAIK, Millwright. Illustrated by numerous wood engravings and two folding plates. 8vo. $5.00

CRISTIANI.—A Technical Treatise on Soap and Candles:
With a Glance at the Industry of Fats and Oils. By R. S. CRISTIANI, Chemist. Author of "Perfumery and Kindred Arts." Illustrated by 176 engravings. 581 pages, 8vo. . . . $7.50

CRISTIANI.—Perfumery and Kindred Arts:
A Comprehensive Treatise on Perfumery, containing a History of Perfumes from the remotest ages to the present time. A complete detailed description of the various Materials and Apparatus used in the Perfumer's Art, with thorough Practical Instruction and careful Formulæ, and advice for the fabrication of all known preparations of the day, including Essences, Tinctures, Extracts, Spirits, Waters, Vinegars, Pomades, Powders, Paints, Oils, Emulsions, Cosmetics, Infusions, Pastilles, Tooth Powders and Washes, Cachous, Hair Dyes, Sachets, Essential Oils, Flavoring Extracts, etc.; and full details for making and manipulating Fancy Toilet Soaps, Shaving Creams, etc., by new and improved methods. With an Appendix giving hints and advice for making and fermenting Domestic Wines, Cordials, Liquors, Candies, Jellies, Syrups, Colors, etc., and for Perfuming and Flavoring Segars, Snuff and Tobacco, and Miscellaneous Receipts for various useful Analogous Articles. By R. S. CRISTIANI, Consulting Chemist and Perfumer, Philadelphia. 8vo. . . $5.00

CROOKES.—A Practical Hand-Book of Dyeing and Calico Printing.
By WM. CROOKES, F. R. S., etc. With eleven page plates, forty-seven specimens of Dyed and Printed Fabrics, and thirty-eight wood cuts. 730 pages, 8vo. $15.00

CROOKES.—Select Methods in Chemical Analysis (chiefly inorganic).
By WM. CROOKES, F. R. S. Illustrated with twenty-two wood cuts. 12mo., 468 pages $5.00

CUPPER.—The Universal Stair-Builder:
Being a new Treatise on the Construction of Stair-Cases and Hand-Rails; showing Plans of the various forms of Stairs, method of Placing the Risers in the Cylinders, general method of describing the Face Moulds for a Hand-Rail, and an expeditious method of Squaring the Rail. Useful also to Stonemasons constructing Stone Stairs and Hand-Rails; with a new method of Sawing the Twist Part of any Hand-Rail square from the face of the plank, and to a parallel width. Also, a new method of forming the Easings of the Rail by a gauge; preceded by some necessary Problems in Practical Geometry, with the Sections of Prismatic Solids. Illustrated by 29 plates. By R. A. CUPPER, Architect, author of "The Practical Stair-Builder's Guide." Third Edition. Large 4to. . $2.50

DAVIDSON.—A Practical Manual of House Painting, Graining, Marbling, and Sign-Writing:
Containing full information on the processes of House Painting in

Oil and Distemper, the Formation of Letters and Practice of Sign-Writing, the Principles of Decorative Art, a Course of Elementary Drawing for House Painters, Writers, etc., and a Collection of Useful Receipts. With nine colored illustrations of Woods and Marbles, and numerous wood engravings. By ELLIS A. DAVIDSON. 12mo. $3.00

DAVIES.—A Treatise on Metalliferous Minerals and Mining:
By D. C. DAVIES, F. G. S., Mining Engineer, Examiner of Mines, Quarries and Collieries. Illustrated by 148 engravings of Geological Formations, Mining Operations and Machinery, drawn from the practice of all parts of the world. 2d Edition, 12mo., 450 pages $5.00

DAVIES.—A Treatise on Slate and Slate Quarrying:
Scientific, Practical and Commercial. By D. C. DAVIES, F. G. S., Mining Engineer, etc. With numerous illustrations and folding plates. 12mo. $2.50

DAWIDOWSKY—BRANNT.—A Practical Treatise on the Fabrication of Glue, Gelatine, Cements, Pastes, Mucilages, etc.:
Comprising a Popular Description of these Industries, based upon Practical Experience. By F. DAWIDOWSKY, Technical Chemist. From the German, with additions, by WILLIAM T. BRANNT. Illustrated. 12mo. (*In preparation.*)

DE GRAFF.—The Geometrical Stair-Builders' Guide:
Being a Plain Practical System of Hand-Railing, embracing all its necessary Details, and Geometrically Illustrated by twenty-two Steel Engravings; together with the use of the most approved principles of Practical Geometry. By SIMON DE GRAFF, Architect. 4to. $2.50

DE KONINCK—DIETZ.—A Practical Manual of Chemical Analysis and Assaying:
As applied to the Manufacture of Iron from its Ores, and to Cast Iron, Wrought Iron, and Steel, as found in Commerce. By L. L. DE KONINCK, Dr. Sc., and E. DIETZ, Engineer. Edited with Notes, by ROBERT MALLET, F. R. S., F. S. G., M. I. C. E., etc. American Edition, Edited with Notes and an Appendix on Iron Ores, by A. A. FESQUET, Chemist and Engineer. 12mo. $2.50

DUNCAN.—Practical Surveyor's Guide:
Containing the necessary information to make any person of common capacity, a finished land surveyor without the aid of a teacher. By ANDREW DUNCAN. Illustrated. 12mo. $1.25

DUPLAIS.—A Treatise on the Manufacture and Distillation of Alcoholic Liquors:
Comprising Accurate and Complete Details in Regard to Alcohol from Wine, Molasses, Beets, Grain, Rice, Potatoes, Sorghum, Asphodel, Fruits, etc.; with the Distillation and Rectification of Brandy, Whiskey, Rum, Gin, Swiss Absinthe, etc., the Preparation of Aromatic Waters, Volatile Oils or Essences, Sugars, Syrups, Aromatic Tinctures, Liqueurs, Cordial Wines, Effervescing Wines, etc., the

Ageing of Brandy and the improvement of Spirits, with Copious Directions and Tables for Testing and Reducing Spirituous Liquors, etc., etc. Translated and Edited from the French of MM. DUPLAIS, Ainè et Jeune. By M. MCKENNIE, M. D. To which are added the United States Internal Revenue Regulations for the Assessment and Collection of Taxes on Distilled Spirits. Illustrated by fourteen folding plates and several wood engravings. 743 pp. 8vo. $10 00

DUSSAUCE.—A General Treatise on the Manufacture of Every Description of Soap:

Comprising the Chemistry of the Art, with Remarks on Alkalies, Saponifiable Fatty Bodies, the apparatus necessary in a Soap Factory, Practical Instructions in the manufacture of the various kinds of Soap, the assay of Soaps, etc., etc. By Prof. H. DUSSAUCE, Chemist. Illustrated. 8vo. $25 00

DUSSAUCE.—A General Treatise on the Manufacture of Vinegar:

Theoretical and Practical. Comprising the various Methods, by the Slow and the Quick Processes, with Alcohol, Wine, Grain, Malt, Cider, Molasses, and Beets; as well as the Fabrication of Wood Vinegar, etc., etc. By Prof. H. DUSSAUCE. 8vo. . $5 00

DUSSAUCE.—A New and Complete Treatise on the Arts of Tanning, Currying, and Leather Dressing:

Comprising all the Discoveries and Improvements made in France, Great Britain, and the United States. Edited from Notes and Documents of Messrs. Sallerou, Grouvelle, Duval, Dessables, Labarraque, Payen, René, De Fontenelle, Malapeyre, etc., etc. By Prof. H. DUSSAUCE, Chemist. Illustrated by 212 wood engravings. 8vo. $25 00

DUSSAUCE.—Practical Treatise on the Fabrication of Matches, Gun Cotton, and Fulminating Powder.

By Professor H. DUSSAUCE. 12mo. $3 00

DYER AND COLOR-MAKER'S COMPANION:

Containing upwards of two hundred Receipts for making Colors, on the most approved principles, for all the various styles and fabrics now in existence; with the Scouring Process, and plain Directions for Preparing, Washing-off, and Finishing the Goods. 12mo. $1 25

EASTON.—A Practical Treatise on Street or Horse-Power Railways:

By ALEXANDER EASTON, C. E. Illustrated by 23 plates. 8vo. $3 00

EDWARDS.—A Catechism of the Marine Steam-Engine,

For the use of Engineers, Firemen, and Mechanics. A Practical Work for Practical Men. By EMORY EDWARDS, Mechanical Engineer. Illustrated by sixty-three Engravings, including examples of the most modern Engines. Third edition, thoroughly revised, with much additional matter. 12mo. 414 pages $2 00

EDWARDS.—Modern American Locomotive Engines,

Their Design, Construction and Management. By EMORY EDWARDS. Illustrated 12mo. $2 00

EDWARDS.—Modern American Marine Engines, Boilers, and Screw Propellers,

Their Design and Construction. Showing the Present Practice of the most Eminent Engineers and Marine Engine Builders in the United States. Illustrated by 30 large and elaborate plates. 4to. $5.00

EDWARDS.—The Practical Steam Engineer's Guide

In the Design, Construction, and Management of American Stationary, Portable, and Steam Fire-Engines, Steam Pumps, Boilers, Injectors, Governors, Indicators, Pistons and Rings, Safety Valves and Steam Gauges. For the use of Engineers, Firemen, and Steam Users. By EMORY EDWARDS. Illustrated by 119 engravings. 420 pages. 12mo. $2 50

ELDER.—Conversations on the Principal Subjects of Political Economy.

By Dr. WILLIAM ELDER. 8vo. $2 50

ELDER.—Questions of the Day,

Economic and Social. By Dr. WILLIAM ELDER. 8vo. . $3 00

ELDER.—Memoir of Henry C. Carey.

By Dr. WILLIAM ELDER. 8vo. cloth. 75

ERNI.—Mineralogy Simplified.

Easy Methods of Determining and Classifying Minerals, including Ores, by means of the Blowpipe, and by Humid Chemical Analysis, based on Professor von Kobell's Tables for the Determination of Minerals, with an Introduction to Modern Chemistry. By HENRY ERNI, A.M., M.D., Professor of Chemistry. Second Edition, rewritten, enlarged and improved. 12mo. (*In press.*)

FITCH.—Bessemer Steel,

Ores and Methods, New Facts and Statistics Relating to the Types of Machinery in Use, the Methods in Vogue, Cost and Class of Labor employed, and the Character and Availability of the Ores utilized in the Manufacture of Bessemer Steel in Europe and in the United States; together with opinions and excerpts from various accepted authorities. Compiled and arranged by THOMAS W. FITCH. 8vo. . $3 00

FLEMING.—Narrow Gauge Railways in America.

A Sketch of their Rise, Progress, and Success. Valuable Statistics as to Grades, Curves, Weight of Rail, Locomotives, Cars, etc. By HOWARD FLEMING. Illustrated, 8vo. $1 50

FORSYTH.—Book of Designs for Headstones, Mural, and other Monuments:

Containing 78 Designs. By JAMES FORSYTH. With an Introduction by CHARLES BOUTELL, M. A. 4 to., cloth . . . $5 00

FRANKEL—HUTTER.—A Practical Treatise on the Manufacture of Starch, Glucose, Starch-Sugar, and Dextrine:

Based on the German of LADISLAUS VON WAGNER, Professor in the Royal Technical High School, Buda-Pest, Hungary, and other authorities. By JULIUS FRANKEL, Graduate of the Polytechnic School of Hanover. Edited by ROBERT HUTTER, Chemist, Practical Manufacturer of Starch-Sugar, Proprietor of the Philadelphia Starch-

Sugar Works. Illustrated by 58 engravings, covering every branch of the subject, including examples of the most recent and best American machinery. 8vo., 344 pp. $3.50

FRAZIER.—Modern Processes in the Metallurgy of Iron and Steel:

By B. W. FRAZIER, Professor of Mining and Metallurgy in Lehigh University, Bethlehem, Pa. Elaborately Illustrated. (*In preparation.*)

GEE.—The Practical Gold Worker:

Or, the Goldsmith's and Jeweller's Instructor in the Art of Alloying, Melting, Reducing, Coloring, Collecting, and Refining; the Processes of Manipulation, Recovery of Waste, Chemical and Physical Properties of Gold, with a New System of Mixing its Alloys, Solders, Enamels, and other Useful Rules and Recipes. By GEORGE E. GEE. 12mo. . , ... $1.75

GEE.—The Silversmith's Handbook:

Containing full instructions for the Alloying and Working of Silver, including the different modes of Refining and Melting the Metal; its Solders; the Preparation of Imitation Alloys; Methods of Manipulation; Prevention of Waste; Instructions for Improving and Finishing the Surface of the Work; together with other Useful Information and Memoranda. By GEORGE E. GEE, Jeweller. Illustrated. 12mo. $1.75

GOTHIC ALBUM FOR CABINET-MAKERS:

Designs for Gothic Furniture. Twenty-three plates. Oblong $2.00

GREGORY.—Mathematics for Practical Men:

Adapted to the Pursuits of Surveyors, Architects, Mechanics, and Civil Engineers. By OLINTHUS GREGORY. 8vo., plates . $3.00

GRIER.—Rural Hydraulics:

A Practical Treatise on Rural Household Water Supply. Giving a full description of Springs and Wells, of Pumps and Hydraulic Ram, with Instructions in Cistern Building, Laying of Pipes, etc. By W. W. GRIER. Illustrated 8vo. 75

GRIMSHAW.—Modern Milling:

Being the substance of two addresses delivered by request, at the Franklin Institute, Philadelphia, January 19th and January 27th, 1881. By ROBERT GRIMSHAW, Ph. D. Edited from the Phonographic Reports. With 28 Illustrations. 8vo. . . . $1.00

GRIMSHAW.—Saws:

The History, Development, Action, Classification, and Comparison of Saws of all kinds. *With Copious Appendices.* Giving the details of Manufacture, Filing, Setting, Gumming, etc. Care and Use of Saws; Tables of Gauges; Capacities of Saw-Mills; List of Saw-Patents, and other valuable information. By ROBERT GRIMSHAW. Second and greatly enlarged edition, *with Supplement*, and 354 Illustrations. Quarto $4.00

GRIMSHAW.—A Supplement to Grimshaw on Saws:

Containing additional practical matter, more especially relating to the

Forms of Saw-Teeth, for special material and conditions, and to the Behavior of Saws under particular conditions. 120 Illustrations. By ROBERT GRIMSHAW. Quarto $2.00

GRISWOLD.—Railroad Engineer's Pocket Companion for the Field:

Comprising Rules for Calculating Deflection Distances and Angles, Tangential Distances and Angles, and all Necessary Tables for Engineers; also the Art of Levelling from Preliminary Survey to the Construction of Railroads, intended Expressly for the Young Engineer, together with Numerous Valuable Rules and Examples. By W. GRISWOLD. 12mo., tucks $1.75

GRUNER.—Studies of Blast Furnace Phenomena:

By M. L. GRUNER, President of the General Council of Mines of France, and lately Professor of Metallurgy at the Ecole des Mines. Translated, with the author's sanction, with an Appendix, by L. D. B. GORDON, F. R. S. E., F. G. S. 8vo. . . . $2.50

GUETTIER.—Metallic Alloys:

Being a Practical Guide to their Chemical and Physical Properties, their Preparation, Composition, and Uses. Translated from the French of A. GUETTIER, Engineer and Director of Founderies, author of "La Fouderie en France," etc., etc. By A. A. FESQUET, Chemist and Engineer. 12mo. $3.00

HASERICK.—The Secrets of the Art of Dyeing Wool, Cotton, and Linen,

Including Bleaching and Coloring Wool and Cotton Hosiery and Random Yarns. A Treatise based on Economy and Practice. By E. C. HASERICK. *Illustrated by 323 Dyed Patterns of the Yarns or Fabrics.* 8vo. $25.00

HATS AND FELTING:

A Practical Treatise on their Manufacture. By a Practical Hatter. Illustrated by Drawings of Machinery, etc. 8vo. . . $1.25

HEINZERLING.—Elements of the Fabrication of Leather,

with Special Regard to the Latest Improvements in this Branch of Industry. A Manual for Tanners, Technologists, Etc. By Dr. Christian Heinzerling. Translated from the German by William T. Brannt, Graduate of the Royal Agricultural College of Eldena, Prussia. With additions by an American Editor. Illustrated by numerous Engravings. 8vo. (*In preparation.*)

HENRY.—The Early and Later History of Petroleum:

With Authentic Facts in regard to its Development in Western Pennsylvania. With Sketches of the Pioneer and Prominent Operators, together with the Refining Capacity of the United States. By J. T. HENRY. Illustrated 8vo. $4.50

HOFFER.—A Practical Treatise on Caoutchouc and Gutta Percha,

Comprising the Properties of the Raw Materials, and the manner of Mixing and Working them; with the Fabrication of Vulcanized and Hard Rubbers, Caoutchouc and Gutta Percha Compositions, Waterproof Substances, Elastic Tissues, the Utilization of Waste, etc., etc. From the German of RAIMUND HOFFER. By W. T. BRANNT. Illustrated 12mo. $2.50

HOFMANN.—A Practical Treatise on the Manufacture of Paper in all its Branches:

By CARL HOFMANN, Late Superintendent of Paper-Mills in Germany and the United States; recently Manager of the "Public Ledger" Paper-Mills, near Elkton, Maryland. Illustrated by 110 wood engravings, and five large Folding Plates. 4to., cloth; about 400 pages $20.00

HUGHES.—American Miller and Millwright's Assistant:

By WILLIAM CARTER HUGHES. 12mo. $1.50

HULME.—Worked Examination Questions in Plane Geometrical Drawing:

For the Use of Candidates for the Royal Military Academy, Woolwich; the Royal Military College, Sandhurst; the Indian Civil Engineering College, Cooper's Hill; Indian Public Works and Telegraph Departments; Royal Marine Light Infantry; the Oxford and Cambridge Local Examinations, etc. By F. EDWARD HULME, F. L. S., F. S. A., Art-Master Marlborough College. Illustrated by 300 examples. Small quarto $3.75

HURST.—A Hand-Book for Architectural Surveyors and others Engaged in Building:

Containing Formulæ useful in Designing Builders' Work, Table of Weights, of the Materials used in Building, Memoranda connected with Builders' Work, Mensuration, the Practice of Builders' Measurement, Contracts of Labor, Valuation of Property, Summary of the Practice in Dilapidation, etc., etc. By J. F. HURST, C. E. Second edition, pocket-book form, full bound $2.00

JERVIS.—Railroad Property:

A Treatise on the Construction and Management of Railways; designed to afford useful knowledge, in the popular style, to the holders of this class of property; as well as Railway Managers, Officers, and Agents. By JOHN B. JERVIS, late Civil Engineer of the Hudson River Railroad, Croton Aqueduct, etc. 12mo., cloth $2.00

KEENE.—A Hand-Book of Practical Gauging:

For the Use of Beginners, to which is added a Chapter on Distillation, describing the process in operation at the Custom-House for ascertaining the Strength of Wines. By JAMES B. KEENE, of H. M. Customs. 8vo. $1.25

KELLEY.—Speeches, Addresses, and Letters on Industrial and Financial Questions:

By HON. WILLIAM D. KELLEY, M. C. 544 pages, 8vo. . $3.00

KELLOGG.—A New Monetary System:

The only means of Securing the respective Rights of Labor and Property, and of Protecting the Public from Financial Revulsions. By EDWARD KELLOGG. Revised from his work on "Labor and other Capital." With numerous additions from his manuscript.

Edited by MARY KELLOGG PUTNAM. Fifth edition. To which is added a Biographical Sketch of the Author. One volume, 12mo.
Paper cover $1.00
Bound in cloth 1.50

KEMLO.—Watch-Repairer's Hand-Book:
Being a Complete Guide to the Young Beginner, in Taking Apart, Putting Together, and Thoroughly Cleaning the English Lever and other Foreign Watches, and all American Watches. By F. KEMLO, Practical Watchmaker. With Illustrations. 12mo. . $1.25

KENTISH.—A Treatise on a Box of Instruments,
And the Slide Rule; with the Theory of Trigonometry and Logarithms, including Practical Geometry, Surveying, Measuring of Timber, Cask and Malt Gauging, Heights, and Distances. By THOMAS KENTISH. In one volume. 12mo. $1.25

KERL.—The Assayer's Manual:
An Abridged Treatise on the Docimastic Examination of Ores, and Furnace and other Artificial Products. By BRUNO KERL, Professor in the Royal School of Mines; Member of the Royal Technical Commission for the Industries, and of the Imperial Patent-Office, Berlin. Translated from the German by WILLIAM T. BRANNT, Graduate of the Royal Agricultural College of Eldena, Prussia. Edited by WILLIAM H. WAHL, Ph. D., Secretary of the Franklin Institute, Philadelphia. Illustrated by sixty-five engravings. 8vo. $3.00

KINGZETT.—The History, Products, and Processes of the Alkali Trade:
Including the most Recent Improvements. By CHARLES THOMAS KINGZETT, Consulting Chemist. With 23 illustrations. 8vo. $2.50

KINSLEY.—Self-Instructor on Lumber Surveying:
For the Use of Lumber Manufacturers, Surveyors, and Teachers. By CHARLES KINSLEY, Practical Surveyor and Teacher of Surveying. 12mo. $2.00

KIRK.—The Founding of Metals:
A Practical Treatise on the Melting of Iron, with a Description of the Founding of Alloys; also, of all the Metals and Mineral Substances used in the Art of Founding. Collected from original sources. By EDWARD KIRK, Practical Foundryman and Chemist. Illustrated. Third edition. 8vo. $2.50

KITTREDGE.—The Compendium of Architectural Sheet-Metal Work:
Profusely Illustrated. Embracing Rules and Directions for Estimates, Items of Cost, Nomenclature, Tables of Brackets, Modillions, Dentals, Trusses, Stop-Blocks, Frieze Pieces, etc. Architect's Specification, Tables of Tin-Roofing, Galvanized Iron, etc., etc. To which is added the Exemplar of Architectural Sheet-Metal Work, containing details of the Centennial Buildings, and other important Sheet-Metal Work, Designs and Prices of Architectural Ornaments, as manufactured for the Trade by the Kittredge Cornice and Ornament Com-

pany, and a Catalogue of Cornices, Window-Caps, Mouldings, etc., as manufactured by the Kittredge Cornice and Ornament Company. The whole supplemented by a full Index and Table of Contents. By A. O. KITTREDGE. 8vo., 565 pages $5.00

LANDRIN.—A Treatise on Steel:
Comprising its Theory, Metallurgy, Properties, Practical Working, and Use. By M. H. C. LANDRIN, JR., Civil Engineer. Translated from the French, with Notes, by A. A. FESQUET, Chemist and Engineer. With an Appendix on the Bessemer and the Martin Processes for Manufacturing Steel, from the Report of Abram S. Hewitt, United States Commissioner to the Universal Exposition, Paris, 1867. 12mo. $3.00

LARDEN.—A School Course on Heat:
By W. LARDEN, M. A. 321 pp. 12mo. $2.00

LARDNER.—The Steam-Engine:
For the Use of Beginners. By DR. LARDNER. Illustrated. 12mo. 75

LARKIN.—The Practical Brass and Iron Founder's Guide:
A Concise Treatise on Brass Founding, Moulding, the Metals and their Alloys, etc.; to which are added Recent Improvements in the Manufacture of Iron, Steel by the Bessemer Process, etc., etc. By JAMES LARKIN, late Conductor of the Brass Foundry Department in Reany, Neafie & Co.'s Penn Works, Philadelphia. Fifth edition, revised, with extensive additions. 12mo. $2.25

LEROUX.—A Practical Treatise on the Manufacture of Worsteds and Carded Yarns:
Comprising Practical Mechanics, with Rules and Calculations applied to Spinning; Sorting, Cleaning, and Scouring Wools; the English and French Methods of Combing, Drawing, and Spinning Worsteds, and Manufacturing Carded Yarns. Translated from the French of CHARLES LEROUX, Mechanical Engineer and Superintendent of a Spinning-Mill, by HORATIO PAINE, M. D., and A. A. FESQUET, Chemist and Engineer. Illustrated by twelve large Plates. To which is added an Appendix, containing Extracts from the Reports of the International Jury, and of the Artisans selected by the Committee appointed by the Council of the Society of Arts, London, on Woolen and Worsted Machinery and Fabrics, as exhibited in the Paris Universal Exposition, 1867. 8vo. $5.00

LEFFEL.—The Construction of Mill-Dams:
Comprising also the Building of Race and Reservoir Embankments and Head-Gates, the Measurement of Streams, Gauging of Water Supply, etc. By JAMES LEFFEL & Co. Illustrated by 58 engravings. 8vo. $2.50

LESLIE.—Complete Cookery:
Directions for Cookery in its Various Branches. By MISS LESLIE. Sixtieth thousand. Thoroughly revised, with the addition of New Receipts. In 12mo., cloth $1.50

LIEBER.—Assayer's Guide:
Or, Practical Directions to Assayers, Miners, and Smelters, for the Tests and Assays, by Heat and by Wet Processes, for the Ores of all the principal Metals, of Gold and Silver Coins and Alloys, and of Coal, etc. By OSCAR M. LIEBER. 12mo. $1.25

LOVE.—The Art of Dyeing, Cleaning, Scouring, and Finishing, on the Most Approved English and French Methods:
Being Practical Instructions in Dyeing Silks, Woolens, and Cottons, Feathers, Chips, Straw, etc. Scouring and Cleaning Bed and Window Curtains, Carpets, Rugs, etc. French and English Cleaning, any Color or Fabric of Silk, Satin, or Damask. By THOMAS LOVE, a Working Dyer and Scourer. Second American Edition, to which are added General Instructions for the use of Aniline Colors. 8vo. 343 pages $5.00

LUKIN.—Amongst Machines:
Embracing Descriptions of the various Mechanical Appliances used in the Manufacture of Wood, Metal, and other Substances. 12mo. $1.75

LUKIN.—The Boy Engineers:
What They Did, and How They Did It. With 30 plates. 18mo. $1.75

LUKIN.—The Young Mechanic:
Practical Carpentry. Containing Directions for the Use of all kinds of Tools, and for Construction of Steam-Engines and Mechanical Models, including the Art of Turning in Wood and Metal. By JOHN LUKIN, Author of "The Lathe and Its Uses," etc. Illustrated. 12mo. $1.75

MAIN and BROWN.—Questions on Subjects Connected with the Marine Steam-Engine:
And Examination Papers; with Hints for their Solution. By THOMAS J. MAIN, Professor of Mathematics, Royal Naval College, and THOMAS BROWN, Chief Engineer, R. N. 12mo., cloth . $1.50

MAIN and BROWN.—The Indicator and Dynamometer:
With their Practical Applications to the Steam-Engine. By THOMAS J. MAIN, M. A. F. R., Ass't S. Professor Royal Naval College, Portsmouth, and THOMAS BROWN, Assoc. Inst. C. E., Chief Engineer R. N., attached to the R. N. College. Illustrated. 8vo. . $1.50

MAIN and BROWN.—The Marine Steam-Engine.
By THOMAS J. MAIN, F. R. Ass't S. Mathematical Professor at the Royal Naval College, Portsmouth, and THOMAS BROWN, Assoc. Inst. C. E., Chief Engineer R. N. Attached to the Royal Naval College. With numerous illustrations. 8vo. . . . $5.00

MARTIN.—Screw-Cutting Tables, for the Use of Mechanical Engineers:
Showing the Proper Arrangement of Wheels for Cutting the Threads of Screws of any Required Pitch; with a Table for Making the Universal Gas-Pipe Thread and Taps. By W. A. MARTIN, Engineer. 8vo. 50

MICHELL.—Mine Drainage:
Being a Complete and Practical Treatise on Direct-Acting Underground Steam Pumping Machinery. With a Description of a large number of the best known Engines, their General Utility and the Special Sphere of their Action, the Mode of their Application, and their Merits compared with other Pumping Machinery. By STEPHEN MICHELL. Illustrated by 137 engravings. 8vo., 277 pages . $6.00

MOLESWORTH.—Pocket-Book of Useful Formulæ and Memoranda for Civil and Mechanical Engineers.
By GUILFORD L. MOLESWORTH, Member of the Institution of Civil Engineers, Chief Resident Engineer of the Ceylon Railway. Full-bound in Pocket-book form $1.00

MOORE.—The Universal Assistant and the Complete Mechanic:
Containing over one million Industrial Facts, Calculations, Receipts, Processes, Trades Secrets, Rules, Business Forms, Legal Items, Etc., in every occupation, from the Household to the Manufactory. By R. MOORE. Illustrated by 500 Engravings. 12mo. . $2.50

MORRIS.—Easy Rules for the Measurement of Earthworks:
By means of the Prismoidal Formula. Illustrated with Numerous Wood-Cuts, Problems, and Examples, and concluded by an Extensive Table for finding the Solidity in cubic yards from Mean Areas. The whole being adapted for convenient use by Engineers, Surveyors, Contractors, and others needing Correct Measurements of Earthwork. By ELWOOD MORRIS, C. E. 8vo. $1.50

MORTON.—The System of Calculating Diameter, Circumference, Area, and Squaring the Circle:
Together with Interest and Miscellaneous Tables, and other information. By JAMES MORTON. Second Edition, enlarged, with the Metric System. 12mo. $1.00

NAPIER.—Manual of Electro-Metallurgy:
Including the Application of the Art to Manufacturing Processes. By JAMES NAPIER. Fourth American, from the Fourth London edition, revised and enlarged. Illustrated by engravings. 8vo. $1.50

NAPIER.—A System of Chemistry Applied to Dyeing.
By JAMES NAPIER, F. C. S. A New and Thoroughly Revised Edition. Completely brought up to the present state of the Science, including the Chemistry of Coal Tar Colors, by A. A. FESQUET, Chemist and Engineer. With an Appendix on Dyeing and Calico Printing, as shown at the Universal Exposition, Paris, 1867. Illustrated. 8vo. 422 pages $5.00

NEVILLE.—Hydraulic Tables, Coefficients, and Formulæ, for finding the Discharge of Water from Orifices, Notches, Weirs, Pipes, and Rivers:
Third Edition, with Additions, consisting of New Formulæ for the Discharge from Tidal and Flood Sluices and Siphons; general information on Rainfall, Catchment-Basins, Drainage, Sewerage, Water Supply for Towns and Mill Power. By JOHN NEVILLE, C. E. M. R.

I. A.; Fellow of the Royal Geological Society of Ireland. Thick 12mo. $3.50

NEWBERY.—Gleanings from Ornamental Art of every style:

Drawn from Examples in the British, South Kensington, Indian, Crystal Palace, and other Museums, the Exhibitions of 1851 and 1862, and the best English and Foreign works. In a series of 100 exquisitely drawn Plates, containing many hundred examples. By ROBERT NEWBERY. 4to. $12.50

NICHOLLS.—The Theoretical and Practical Boiler-Maker and Engineer's Reference Book:

Containing a variety of Useful Information for Employers of Labor, Foremen and Working Boiler-Makers, Iron, Copper, and Tinsmiths, Draughtsmen, Engineers, the General Steam-using Public, and for the Use of Science Schools and Classes. By SAMUEL NICHOLLS. Illustrated by sixteen plates, 12mo. $2.50

NICHOLSON.—A Manual of the Art of Bookbinding:

Containing full instructions in the different Branches of Forwarding, Gilding, and Finishing. Also, the Art of Marbling Book-edges and Paper. By JAMES B. NICHOLSON. Illustrated. 12mo., cloth $2.25

NICOLLS.—The Railway Builder:

A Hand-Book for Estimating the Probable Cost of American Railway Construction and Equipment. By WILLIAM J. NICOLLS, Civil Engineer. Illustrated, full bound, pocket-book form . $2.00

NORMANDY.—The Commercial Handbook of Chemical Analysis:

Or Practical Instructions for the Determination of the Intrinsic or Commercial Value of Substances used in Manufactures, in Trades, and in the Arts. By A. NORMANDY. New Edition, Enlarged, and to a great extent rewritten. By HENRY M. NOAD, Ph.D., F.R.S., thick 12mo. $5.00

NORRIS.—A Handbook for Locomotive Engineers and Machinists:

Comprising the Proportions and Calculations for Constructing Locomotives; Manner of Setting Valves; Tables of Squares, Cubes, Areas, etc., etc. By SEPTIMUS NORRIS, M. E. New edition. Illustrated, 12mo. $1.50

NORTH.—The Practical Assayer:

Containing Easy Methods for the Assay of the Principal Metals and Alloys. Principally designed for explorers and those interested in Mines. By OLIVER NORTH. Illustrated. 12mo. . $2.50

NYSTROM.—A New Treatise on Elements of Mechanics:

Establishing Strict Precision in the Meaning of Dynamical Terms: accompanied with an Appendix on Duodenal Arithmetic and Metrology. By JOHN W. NYSTROM, C. E. Illustrated. 8vo. $2.00

NYSTROM.—On Technological Education and the Construction of Ships and Screw Propellers:

For Naval and Marine Engineers. By JOHN W. NYSTROM, late

Acting Chief Engineer, U. S. N. Second edition, revised, with additional matter. Illustrated by seven engravings. 12mo. . $1.50

O'NEILL.—A Dictionary of Dyeing and Calico Printing:
Containing a brief account of all the Substances and Processes in use in the Art of Dyeing and Printing Textile Fabrics; with Practical Receipts and Scientific Information. By CHARLES O'NEILL, Analytical Chemist. To which is added an Essay on Coal Tar Colors and their application to Dyeing and Calico Printing. By A. A. FESQUET, Chemist and Engineer. With an appendix on Dyeing and Calico Printing, as shown at the Universal Exposition, Paris, 1867. 8vo., 491 pages $5.00

ORTON.—Underground Treasures:
How and Where to Find Them. A Key for the Ready Determination of all the Useful Minerals within the United States. By JAMES ORTON, A.M., Late Professor of Natural History in Vassar College, N. Y.; Cor. Mem. of the Academy of Natural Sciences, Philadelphia, and of the Lyceum of Natural History, New York; author of the "Andes and the Amazon," etc. A New Edition, with Additions. Illustrated $1.50

OSBORN.—The Metallurgy of Iron and Steel:
Theoretical and Practical in all its Branches; with special reference to American Materials and Processes. By H. S. OSBORN, LL. D., Professor of Mining and Metallurgy in Lafayette College, Easton, Pennsylvania. Illustrated by numerous large folding plates and wood-engravings. 8vo. $25.00

OVERMAN.—The Manufacture of Steel:
Containing the Practice and Principles of Working and Making Steel. A Handbook for Blacksmiths and Workers in Steel and Iron, Wagon Makers, Die Sinkers, Cutlers, and Manufacturers of Files and Hardware, of Steel and Iron, and for Men of Science and Art. By FREDERICK OVERMAN, Mining Engineer, Author of the "Manufacture of Iron," etc. A new, enlarged, and revised Edition. By A. A. FESQUET, Chemist and Engineer. 12mo. . . . $1.50

OVERMAN.—The Moulder's and Founder's Pocket Guide:
A Treatise on Moulding and Founding in Green-sand, Dry-sand, Loam, and Cement; the Moulding of Machine Frames, Mill-gear, Hollow-ware, Ornaments, Trinkets, Bells, and Statues; Description of Moulds for Iron, Bronze, Brass, and other Metals; Plaster of Paris, Sulphur, Wax, etc.; the Construction of Melting Furnaces, the Melting and Founding of Metals; the Composition of Alloys and their Nature, etc., etc. By FREDERICK OVERMAN, M. E. A new Edition, to which is added a Supplement on Statuary and Ornamental Moulding, Ordnance, Malleable Iron Castings, etc. By A. A. FESQUET, Chemist and Engineer. Illustrated by 44 engravings. 12mo. . $2.00

PAINTER, GILDER, AND VARNISHER'S COMPANION:
Containing Rules and Regulations in everything relating to the Arts of Painting, Gilding, Varnishing, Glass-Staining, Graining, Marbling, Sign-Writing, Gilding on Glass, and Coach Painting and Varnishing;

Tests for the Detection of Adulterations in Oils, Colors, etc.; and a Statement of the Diseases to which Painters are peculiarly liable, with the Simplest and Best Remedies. Sixteenth Edition. Revised, with an Appendix. Containing Colors and Coloring—Theoretical and Practical. Comprising descriptions of a great variety of Additional Pigments, their Qualities and Uses, to which are added, Dryers, and Modes and Operations of Painting, etc. Together with Chevreul's Principles of Harmony and Contrast of Colors. 12mo. Cloth $1.50

PALLETT.—The Miller's, Millwright's, and Engineer's Guide.

By HENRY PALLETT. Illustrated. 12mo. $3.00

PEARSE.—A Concise History of the Iron Manufacture of the American Colonies up to the Revolution, and of Pennsylvania until the present time.

By JOHN B. PEARSE. Illustrated 12mo. $2.00

PERCY.—The Manufacture of Russian Sheet-Iron.

By JOHN PERCY, M. D., F. R. S., Lecturer on Metallurgy at the Royal School of Mines, and to The Advance Class of Artillery Officers at the Royal Artillery Institution, Woolwich; Author of "Metallurgy." With Illustrations. 8vo., paper . . 50 cts.

PERKINS.—Gas and Ventilation:

Practical Treatise on Gas and Ventilation. With Special Relation to Illuminating, Heating, and Cooking by Gas. Including Scientific Helps to Engineer-students and others. With Illustrated Diagrams. By E. E. PERKINS. 12mo., cloth $1.25

PERKINS AND STOWE.—A New Guide to the Sheet-iron and Boiler Plate Roller:

Containing a Series of Tables showing the Weight of Slabs and Piles to Produce Boiler Plates, and of the Weight of Piles and the Sizes of Bars to produce Sheet-iron; the Thickness of the Bar Gauge in decimals; the Weight per foot, and the Thickness on the Bar or Wire Gauge of the fractional parts of an inch; the Weight per sheet, and the Thickness on the Wire Gauge of Sheet-iron of various dimensions to weigh 112 lbs. per bundle; and the conversion of Short Weight into Long Weight, and Long Weight into Short. Estimated and collected by G. H. PERKINS and J. G. STOWE. $2.50

POWELL—CHANCE—HARRIS.—The Principles of Glass Making.

By HARRY J. POWELL, B. A. Together with Treatises on Crown and Sheet Glass; by HENRY CHANCE, M. A. And Plate Glass, by H. G. HARRIS, Asso. M. Inst. C. E. Illustrated 18mo. . $1.50

PROTEAUX.—Practical Guide for the Manufacture of Paper and Boards.

By A. PROTEAUX. From the French, by HORATIO PAINE, A. B., M. D. To which is added the Manufacture of Paper from Wood, by HENRY T. BROWN. Illustrated by six plates. 8vo. . $12.50

PROCTOR.—A Pocket-Book of Useful Tables and Formulæ for Marine Engineers.

By FRANK PROCTOR. Second Edition, Revised and Enlarged. Full bound pocket-book form $1.50

REGNAULT.—Elements of Chemistry.

By M. V. REGNAULT. Translated from the French by T. FORREST BETTON, M. D., and edited, with Notes, by JAMES C. BOOTH, Melter and Refiner U. S. Mint, and WILLIAM L. FABER, Metallurgist and Mining Engineer. Illustrated by nearly 700 wood engravings. Comprising nearly 1,500 pages. In two volumes, 8vo., cloth . $7.50

ROPER.—A Catechism of High-Pressure, or Non-Condensing Steam-Engines:

Including the Modelling, Constructing, and Management of Steam-Engines and Steam Boilers. With valuable illustrations. By STEPHEN ROPER, Engineer. Sixteenth edition, revised and enlarged. 18mo., tucks, gilt edge $2.00

ROPER.—Engineer's Handy-Book:

Containing a full Explanation of the Steam-Engine Indicator, and its Use and Advantages to Engineers and Steam Users. With Formulæ for Estimating the Power of all Classes of Steam-Engines; also, Facts, Figures, Questions, and Tables for Engineers who wish to qualify themselves for the United States Navy, the Revenue Service, the Mercantile Marine, or to take charge of the Better Class of Stationary Steam-Engines. Sixth edition. 16mo., 690 pages, tucks, gilt edge $3.50

ROPER.—Hand-Book of Land and Marine Engines:

Including the Modelling, Construction, Running, and Management of Land and Marine Engines and Boilers. With illustrations. By STEPHEN ROPER, Engineer. Sixth edition. 12mo., tucks, gilt edge. $3.50

ROPER.—Hand-Book of the Locomotive:

Including the Construction of Engines and Boilers, and the Construction, Management, and Running of Locomotives. By STEPHEN ROPER. Eleventh edition. 18mo., tucks, gilt edge . $2.50

ROPER.—Hand-Book of Modern Steam Fire-Engines.

With illustrations. By STEPHEN ROPER, Engineer. Fourth edition, 12mo., tucks, gilt edge $3.50

ROPER.—Questions and Answers for Engineers.

This little book contains all the Questions that Engineers will be asked when undergoing an Examination for the purpose of procuring Licenses, and they are so plain that any Engineer or Fireman of ordinary intelligence may commit them to memory in a short time. By STEPHEN ROPER, Engineer. Third edition . . . $3.00

ROPER.—Use and Abuse of the Steam Boiler.

By STEPHEN ROPER, Engineer. Eighth edition, with illustrations. 18mo., tucks, gilt edge $2.00

ROSE.—The Complete Practical Machinist:

Embracing Lathe-Work, Vise-Work, Drills and Drilling, Taps and Dies, Hardening and Tempering, the Making and Use of Tools, Tool Grinding, Marking Out Work, etc. By JOSHUA ROSE, Author of "The Pattern-maker's Assistant" and "The Slide Valve." Illustrated by 196 engravings. Eighth edition, revised and enlarged by the addition of much new matter. 12mo., 441 pages . . . $2.50

ROSE.—Mechanical Drawing Self-Taught:

Comprising Instructions in the Selection and Preparation of Drawing Instruments, Elementary Instruction in Practical Mechanical Drawing, together with Examples in Simple Geometry and Elementary Mechanism, including Screw Threads, Gear Wheels, Mechanical Motions, Engines and Boilers. By JOSHUA ROSE, M. E., Author of "The Complete Practical Machinist," "The Pattern-maker's Assistant," "The Slide-valve." Illustrated by 330 engravings. 8vo., 313 pages $4.00

ROSE.—The Slide-Valve Practically Explained:

Embracing simple and complete Practical Demonstrations of the operation of each element in a Slide-valve Movement, and illustrating the effects of Variations in their Proportions by examples carefully selected from the most recent and successful practice. By JOSHUA ROSE, M. E., Author of "The Complete Practical Machinist," "The Pattern-maker's Assistant," etc. Illustrated by 35 engravings $1.00

ROSELEUR.—Galvanoplastic Manipulations:

A Practical Guide for the Gold and Silver Electroplater, and the Galvanoplastic Operator. By ALFRED ROSELEUR, Chemist, Professor of the Galvanoplastic Art, Gold and Silver Electroplater. Edited from the fourth French edition, with the addition of much new and original American matter, bringing it up to the best practice of the present day. By WILLIAM H. WAHL, Ph. D., Secretary of the Franklin Institute. Illustrated by about 200 engravings. (*In press.*)

SHAW.—Civil Architecture:

Being a Complete Theoretical and Practical System of Building, containing the Fundamental Principles of the Art. By EDWARD SHAW, Architect. To which is added a Treatise on Gothic Architecture, etc. By THOMAS W. SILLOWAY and GEORGE M. HARDING, Architects. The whole illustrated by 102 quarto plates finely engraved on copper. Eleventh edition. 4to. $10.00

SHUNK.—A Practical Treatise on Railway Curves and Location, for Young Engineers.

By WILLIAM F. SHUNK, Civil Engineer. 12mo. Full bound pocket-book form $2.00

SLATER.—The Manual of Colors and Dye Wares.

By J. W. SLATER. 12mo. $3.75

SLOAN.—American Houses:

A variety of Original Designs for Rural Buildings. Illustrated by twenty-six colored Engravings, with Descriptive References. By SAMUEL SLOAN, Architect, author of the "Model Architect," etc. etc. 8vo. $1.50

SLOAN.—Homestead Architecture:

Containing Forty Designs for Villas, Cottages, and Farm-houses, with Essays on Style, Construction, Landscape Gardening, Furniture, etc., etc. Illustrated by upwards of 200 engravings. By SAMUEL SLOAN, Architect. 8vo. $3.50

SMEATON.—Builder's Pocket-Companion:
Containing the Elements of Building, Surveying, and Architecture; with Practical Rules and Instructions connected with the subject. By A. C. SMEATON, Civil Engineer, etc. 12mo. $1.50

SMITH.—A Manual of Political Economy.
By E. PESHINE SMITH. A new Edition, to which is added a full Index. 12mo. $1.25

SMITH.—Parks and Pleasure-Grounds:
Or Practical Notes on Country Residences, Villas, Public Parks, and Gardens. By CHARLES H. J. SMITH, Landscape Gardener and Garden Architect, etc., etc. 12mo. $2.00

SMITH.—The Dyer's Instructor:
Comprising Practical Instructions in the Art of Dyeing Silk, Cotton, Wool, and Worsted, and Woolen Goods; containing nearly 800 Receipts. To which is added a Treatise on the Art of Padding; and the Printing of Silk Warps, Skeins, and Handkerchiefs, and the various Mordants and Colors for the different styles of such work. By DAVID SMITH, Pattern Dyer. 12mo. $3.00

SMYTH.—A Rudimentary Treatise on Coal and Coal-Mining.
By WARRINGTON W. SMYTH, M. A., F. R. G., President R. G. S. of Cornwall. Fifth edition, revised and corrected. With numerous illustrations. 12mo. $1.75

SNIVELY.—A Treatise on the Manufacture of Perfumes and Kindred Toilet Articles.
By JOHN H. SNIVELY, Phr. D., Professor of Analytical Chemistry in the Tennessee College of Pharmacy. 8vo. $3.00

SNIVELY.—Tables for Systematic Qualitative Chemical Analysis.
By JOHN H. SNIVELY, Phr. D. 8vo. $1.00

SNIVELY.—The Elements of Systematic Qualitative Chemical Analysis:
A Hand-book for Beginners. By JOHN H. SNIVELY, Phr. D. 16mo. $2.00

STEWART.—The American System:
Speeches on the Tariff Question, and on Internal Improvements, principally delivered in the House of Representatives of the United States. By ANDREW STEWART, late M. C. from Pennsylvania. With a Portrait, and a Biographical Sketch. 8vo. . . . $3.00

STOKES.—The Cabinet-Maker and Upholsterer's Companion:
Comprising the Art of Drawing, as applicable to Cabinet Work; Veneering, Inlaying, and Buhl-Work; the Art of Dyeing and Staining Wood, Ivory, Bone, Tortoise-Shell, etc. Directions for Lackering, Japanning, and Varnishing; to make French Polish, Glues, Cements, and Compositions; with numerous Receipts, useful to workmen generally. By J. STOKES. Illustrated. A New Edition, with an Appendix upon French Polishing, Staining, Imitating, Varnishing, etc., etc. 12mo. $1.25

STRENGTH AND OTHER PROPERTIES OF METALS:
Reports of Experiments on the Strength and other Properties of Metals for Cannon. With a Description of the Machines for Testing Metals, and of the Classification of Cannon in service. By Officers of the Ordnance Department, U. S. Army. By authority of the Secretary of War. Illustrated by 25 large steel plates. Quarto . $10.00

SULLIVAN.—Protection to Native Industry.
By Sir EDWARD SULLIVAN, Baronet, author of "Ten Chapters on Social Reforms." 8vo. $1.50

SYME.—Outlines of an Industrial Science.
By DAVID SYME. 12mo. $2.00

TABLES SHOWING THE WEIGHT OF ROUND, SQUARE, AND FLAT BAR IRON, STEEL, ETC.,
By Measurement. Cloth 63

TAYLOR.—Statistics of Coal:
Including Mineral Bituminous Substances employed in Arts and Manufactures; with their Geographical, Geological, and Commercial Distribution and Amount of Production and Consumption on the American Continent. With Incidental Statistics of the Iron Manufacture. By R. C. TAYLOR. Second edition, revised by S. S. HALDEMAN. Illustrated by five Maps and many wood engravings. 8vo., cloth $10.00

TEMPLETON.—The Practical Examinator on Steam and the Steam-Engine:
With Instructive References relative thereto, arranged for the Use of Engineers, Students, and others. By WILLIAM TEMPLETON, Engineer. 12mo. $1.25

THAUSING.—The Theory and Practice of the Preparation of Malt and the Fabrication of Beer:
With especial reference to the Vienna Process of Brewing. Elaborated from personal experience by JULIUS E. THAUSING, Professor at the School for Brewers, and at the Agricultural Institute, Mödling, near Vienna. Translated from the German by WILLIAM T. BRANNT, Graduate of the Royal Agricultural College of Eldena, Prussia. Thoroughly and elaborately edited, with much American matter, and according to the latest and most Scientific Practice, by A. SCHWARZ, Graduate of the Polytechnic School in Prague, Director of the First Scientific Station for Brewing in the United States, Publisher of "The American Brewer," and Dr. A. H. BAUER, M. A. C. S., Analytical Chemist, and Superintendent of the above Station, Editor of "The American Brewer." Illustrated by 140 engravings. 8vo. 815 pages $10.00

THOMAS.—The Modern Practice of Photography.
By R. W. THOMAS, F. C. S. 8vo. 75

THOMPSON.—Political Economy. With Especial Reference to the Industrial History of Nations.
By ROBERT E. THOMPSON, M. A., Professor of Social Science in the University of Pennsylvania. 12mo. $1.50

TURNER'S (THE) COMPANION:

Containing Instructions in Concentric, Elliptic, and Eccentric Turning; also various Plates of Chucks, Tools, and Instruments; and Directions for using the Eccentric Cutter, Drill, Vertical Cutter, and Circular Rest; with Patterns and Instructions for working them. 12mo. $1.25

TURNING: Specimens of Fancy Turning Executed on the Hand or Foot-Lathe:

With Geometric, Oval, and Eccentric Chucks, and Elliptical Cutting Frame. By an Amateur. Illustrated by 30 exquisite Photographs. 4to. $3.00

URBIN—BRULL.—A Practical Guide for Puddling Iron and Steel.

By ED. URBIN, Engineer of Arts and Manufactures. A Prize Essay, read before the Association of Engineers, Graduate of the School of Mines, of Liege, Belgium, at the Meeting of 1865–6. To which is added A COMPARISON OF THE RESISTING PROPERTIES OF IRON AND STEEL. By A. BRULL. Translated from the French by A. A. FESQUET, Chemist and Engineer. 8vo. $1.00

VAILE.—Galvanized-Iron Cornice-Worker's Manual:

Containing Instructions in Laying out the Different Mitres, and Making Patterns for all kinds of Plain and Circular Work. Also, Tables of Weights, Areas and Circumferences of Circles, and other Matter calculated to Benefit the Trade. By CHARLES A. VAILE. Illustrated by twenty-one plates. 4to. $5.00

VILLE.—On Artificial Manures:

Their Chemical Selection and Scientific Application to Agriculture. A series of Lectures given at the Experimental Farm at Vincennes, during 1867 and 1874–75. By M. GEORGES VILLE. Translated and Edited by WILLIAM CROOKES, F. R. S. Illustrated by thirty-one engravings. 8vo., 450 pages $6.00

VILLE.—The School of Chemical Manures:

Or, Elementary Principles in the Use of Fertilizing Agents. From the French of M. GEO. VILLE, by A. A. FESQUET, Chemist and Engineer. With Illustrations. 12mo. $1.25

VOGDES.—The Architect's and Builder's Pocket-Companion and Price-Book:

Consisting of a Short but Comprehensive Epitome of Decimals, Duodecimals, Geometry, and Mensuration; with Tables of U. S. Measures, Sizes, Weights, Strengths, etc., of Iron, Wood, Stone, and various other Materials, Quantities of Materials in Given Sizes, and Dimensions of Wood, Brick, and Stone; and a full and complete Bill of Prices for Carpenter's Work; also, Rules for Computing and Valuing Brick and Brick Work, Stone Work, Painting, Plastering, etc. By FRANK W. VOGDES, Architect. Illustrated. Full bound in pocket-book form $2.00
Bound in cloth 1.50

WARE.—The Sugar Beet.

Including a History of the Beet Sugar Industry in Europe, Varieties of the Sugar Beet, Examination, Soils, Tillage, Seeds and Sowing, Yield and Cost of Cultivation, Harvesting, Transportation, Conservation, Feeding Qualities of the Beet and of the Pulp, etc. By LEWIS S. WARE, C. E., M. E. Illustrated by ninety engravings. 8vo. $4.00

WARN.—The Sheet-Metal Worker's Instructor:

For Zinc, Sheet-Iron, Copper, and Tin-Plate Workers, etc. Containing a selection of Geometrical Problems; also, Practical and Simple Rules for Describing the various Patterns required in the different branches of the above Trades. By REUBEN H. WARN, Practical Tin-Plate Worker. To which is added an Appendix, containing Instructions for Boiler-Making, Mensuration of Surfaces and Solids, Rules for Calculating the Weights of different Figures of Iron and Steel, Tables of the Weights of Iron, Steel, etc. Illustrated by thirty-two Plates and thirty-seven Wood Engravings. 8vo. . $3.00

WARNER.—New Theorems, Tables, and Diagrams, for the Computation of Earth-work:

Designed for the use of Engineers in Preliminary and Final Estimates, of Students in Engineering, and of Contractors and other non-professional Computers. In two parts, with an Appendix. Part I. A Practical Treatise; Part II. A Theoretical Treatise, and the Appendix. Containing Notes to the Rules and Examples of Part I.; Explanations of the Construction of Scales, Tables, and Diagrams, and a Treatise upon Equivalent Square Bases and Equivalent Level Heights. The whole illustrated by numerous original engravings, comprising explanatory cuts for Definitions and Problems, Stereometric Scales and Diagrams, and a series of Lithographic Drawings from Models: Showing all the Combinations of Solid Forms which occur in Railroad Excavations and Embankments. By JOHN WARNER, A. M., Mining and Mechanical Engineer. Illustrated by 14 Plates. A new, revised and improved edition. 8vo. $4.00

WATSON.—A Manual of the Hand-Lathe:

Comprising Concise Directions for Working Metals of all kinds, Ivory, Bone and Precious Woods; Dyeing, Coloring, and French Polishing; Inlaying by Veneers, and various methods practised to produce Elaborate work with Dispatch, and at Small Expense. By EGBERT P. WATSON, Author of "The Modern Practice of American Machinists and Engineers." Illustrated by 78 engravings. $1.50

WATSON.—The Modern Practice of American Machinists and Engineers:

Including the Construction, Application, and Use of Drills, Lathe Tools, Cutters for Boring Cylinders, and Hollow-work generally, with the most Economical Speed for the same; the Results verified by Actual Practice at the Lathe, the Vise, and on the Floor. Together with Workshop Management, Economy of Manufacture, the Steam-Engine, Boilers, Gears, Belting, etc., etc. By EGBERT P. WATSON. Illustrated by eighty-six engravings. 12mo. $2.50

WATSON.—The Theory and Practice of the Art of Weaving by Hand and Power:

With Calculations and Tables for the Use of those connected with the Trade. By JOHN WATSON, Manufacturer and Practical Machine-Maker. Illustrated by large Drawings of the best Power Looms. 8vo. $7.50

WEATHERLY.—Treatise on the Art of Boiling Sugar, Crystallizing, Lozenge-making, Comfits, Gum Goods,

And other processes for Confectionery, etc., in which are explained, in an easy and familiar manner, the various Methods of Manufacturing every Description of Raw and Refined Sugar Goods, as sold by Confectioners and others. 12mo. $1.50

WEDDING.—Elements of the Metallurgy of Iron.

By Dr. HERMANN WEDDING, Royal Privy Counsellor of Mines, Berlin, Prussia. Translated from the second revised and rewritten German edition. By WILLIAM T. BRANNT, Graduate of the Royal Agricultural College at Eldena, Prussia. Edited by WILLIAM H. WAHL, Ph. D., Secretary of the Franklin Institute, Philadelphia. Illustrated by about 250 engravings. 8vo., about 500 pages (*In preparation.*) . . . .

WEINHOLD.—Introduction to Experimental Physics, Theoretical and Practical.

Including directions for Constructing Physical Apparatus and for Making Experiments. By ADOLF F. WEINHOLD, Professor in the Royal Technical School at Chemnitz. Translated and edited, with the author's sanction, by BENJAMIN LOEWY, F. R. A. S., with a preface, by G. C. FOSTER, F. R. S. Illustrated by three colored plates and 404 wood-cuts. 8vo., 848 pages $6.00

WILL.—Tables of Qualitative Chemical Analysis.

With an Introductory Chapter on the Course of Analysis. By Professor HEINRICH WILL, of Giessen, Germany. Third American, from the eleventh German edition. Edited by CHARLES F. HIMES, Ph. D., Professor of Natural Science, Dickinson College, Carlisle, Pa. 8vo. $1.50

WILLIAMS.—On Heat and Steam:

Embracing New Views of Vaporization, Condensation, and Explosion. By CHARLES WYE WILLIAMS, A. I. C. E. Illustrated 8vo. $3 50

WILSON.—A Treatise on Steam Boilers:

Their Strength, Construction, and Economical Working. By ROBERT WILSON. Illustrated 12mo. $2.50

WILSON.—Cotton Carder's Companion:

In which is given a description of the manner of Picking, Baling, Marketing, Opening, and Carding Cotton; to which is added a list of valuable Tables, Rules, and Receipts, by FOSTER WILSON. 12mo. $1.50

WILSON.—First Principles of Political Economy:
With Reference to Statesmanship and the Progress of Civilization. By Professor W. D. WILSON, of the Cornell University. A new and revised edition. 12mo. $1.50

WOHLER.—A Hand-book of Mineral Analysis.
By F. WÖHLER, Professor of Chemistry in the University of Göttingen. Edited by HENRY B. NASON, Professor of Chemistry in the Renssalaer Polytechnic Institute, Troy, New York. Illustrated 12mo. $3.00

WORSSAM.—On Mechanical Saws:
From the Transactions of the Society of Engineers, 1869. By S. W. WORSSAM, JR. Illustrated by eighteen large plates. 8vo. . $2.50

FAIRBAIRN.—The Principles of Mechanism and Machinery of Transmission:
Comprising the Principles of Mechanism, Wheels, and Pulleys, Strength and Proportion of Shafts, Coupling of Shafts, and Engaging and Disengaging Gear. By SIR WILLIAM FAIRBAIRN, Bart. C. E. Beautifully illustrated by over 150 wood-cuts. In one volume, 12mo $2.50

RIFFAULT, VERGNAUD, and TOUSSAINT.—A Practical Treatise on the Manufacture of Colors for Painting:
Comprising the Origin, Definition, and Classification of Colors; the Treatment of the Raw Materials; the best Formulæ and the Newest Processes for the Preparation of every description of Pigment, and the Necessary Apparatus and Directions for its Use; Dryers; the Testing, Application, and Qualities of Paints, etc., etc. By MM. RIFFAULT, VERGNAUD, and TOUSSAINT. Revised and Edited by M. F. MALEPEYRE. Translated from the French, by A. A. FESQUET, Chemist and Engineer. Illustrated by Eighty engravings. In one vol., 8vo., 659 pages $7.50

THOMSON.—Freight Charges Calculator:
By ANDREW THOMSON, Freight Agent. 24mo. . . $1.25
This useful little volume comprises Tables for the Calculation of Freight at all prices per 100 lbs. *from one cent to one dollar.*

WIGHTWICK.—Hints to Young Architects:
Comprising Advice to those who, while yet at school, are destined to the Profession; to such as, having passed their pupilage, are about to travel; and to those who, having completed their education, are about to practise. Together with a Model Specification involving a great variety of instructive and suggestive matter. By GEORGE WIGHTWICK, Architect. A new edition, revised and considerably enlarged; comprising Treatises on the Principles of Construction and Design. By G. HUSKISSON GUILLAUME, Architect. Numerous Illustrations. One vol. 12mo. $2.00

www.ingramcontent.com/pod-product-compliance
Lightning Source LLC
LaVergne TN
LVHW012326100826
845148LV00017B/350

* 9 7 8 1 4 2 5 5 2 1 2 2 6 *